So you really want t

French Prep

BOOK 2
Answer Book

Nigel Pearce, B.A., M.I.L.

Editor: Joyce Capek

www.galorepark.co.uk

Published by Galore Park Publishing Ltd
19/21 Sayers Lane, Tenterden, Kent TN30 6BW
www.galorepark.co.uk

Text copyright © Nigel Pearce 2006

The right of Nigel Pearce to be identified as the author of this Work has been asserted by him in accordance with sections 77 and 78 of the Copyright, Designs and Patents Act 1988.

Typography by Typematter, Basingstoke
Printed and bound in the UK by Antony Rowe Ltd, Chippenham

ISBN-13 978 1 902984 65 0
ISBN-1 902984 65 X

All rights reserved: no part of this publication may be reproduced, stored in a retrieval system, or transmitted in any form or by any means, electronic, mechanical, photocopying, recording or otherwise, without either the prior written permission of the copyright owner or a licence permitting restricted copying issued by the Copyright Licensing Agency, 90 Tottenham Court Road, London W1P 0LP.

First published 2006

Also available:
Pupil's book   ISBN-10: 1 902984 51 X
Audio CD   ISBN-10: 1 902984 52 8
Assessment pack   ISBN-10: 1 902984 88 9

Also available in the *So You Really Want to Learn* series:
English Prep
Latin
Latin Prep
Maths Prep
Science Prep
Spanish

Preface

This book contains a complete set of answers to all the exercises in *So you really want to learn French Prep Book 2*, including translations of all the passages. These answers are not intended to be prescriptive but should provide guidance to those using the course.

Further assessment material to accompany this course is also available, which may be used at the end of each chapter. This material consists of worksheets and audio material on a single CD and complements the work of the pupil's book. It has been designed to meet the requirements of pupils preparing for the Common Entrance examination but may prove useful as a means of assessing the progress of anyone using this course. It is available on a multi-format CD (ISBN-13 978 1 902984 8 89) with the worksheets stored in PDF format, allowing users to print off and copy these as required.

NJP
April 2006

Chapitre 1

The four seasons

In spring, Georges and Martine like to walk the dog. In summer, they like to go to the beach. In the autumn, they play boules in the village. In winter, the whole family goes skiing in the Alps.

Exercice 1.1 – CD: 1

Martine.   What do you like to do in spring?
Georges.   I like to walk the dog and play rugby with friends.
Martine.   I don't like rugby. It's dangerous!
Georges.   When the weather's nice we can go for long walks.
Martine.   Yes. I like to go climbing.
Georges.   But climbing, that's dangerous too!

1. He that he likes to walk the dog and play rugby with friends.
2. She thinks rugby's dangerous.
3. She likes to go climbing then.
4. He says that climbing is dangerous too.

Exercice 1.2 – CD: 2

Martine.   What's your favourite season? Do you like the summer?
Georges.   Oh yes. I love the summer. In summer we go on holiday to the seaside...
Claire.   That's true. We can sunbathe or go swimming.
Jean-Pierre.   You like that? I prefer to go windsurfing.

1. Au printemps, Georges et Martine **aiment** promener le chien.
2. En été, Claire **aime** se baigner à la plage.
3. Georges adore l'été, parce qu'on **va** en vacances.
4. Au printemps, Georges **joue** au rugby avec ses copains.
5. Jean-Pierre **préfère** faire de la planche à voile.

Exercice 1.3

1. Il fait très froid.
2. Il pleut.
3. Il fait beau.
4. Il y a des nuages.
5. Il y a du soleil. / Il fait du soleil.
6. Il fait très chaud.
7. Il fait du vent.
8. Il fait du brouillard.
9. Il pleut. / Il pleut beaucoup.
10. Il neige.

Exercice 1.4

1. Vrai.
2. Faux. Il pleut à Manchester.
3. Faux. A Cardiff, il ne fait pas 30° en décembre.
4. Vrai.
5. Vrai.
6. Vrai.
7. Faux. Dans le désert il ne pleut pas beaucoup.
8. Faux. En hiver, il fait froid en Ecosse.
9. Vrai.
10. Faux. Il neige souvent en Suisse.

Exercice 1.5

1. Il fait du soleil aujourd'hui, mais il fait froid.
2. En été, il fait chaud.
3. En automne, il fait beau, mais il ne fait pas chaud.
4. En hiver, il neige et il fait froid.
5. Il ne neige pas souvent en Afrique.
6. Il fait bon, mais il ne fait pas très chaud.
7. En France, il neige quelquefois.
8. Quelquefois, il fait assez chaud.
9. Il fait froid aujourd'hui.
10. Au printemps, il fait assez froid.

Exercice 1.6

1. It is warm (hot) and fine.
2. It is sunny.
3. In England, the weather is sometimes fine.
4. It is raining, but it is quite hot.
5. It's very cold today.
6. In Switzerland, it snows in the spring.
7. It isn't cold in summer.
8. We play tennis when it is fine.
9. Put on your jumper – it's chilly.
10. It is windy in autumn.

Exercice 1.7 – CD: 3

In March, Monsieur Banane goes to the market on Fridays. In summer, there is a market in his village twice a week, on Fridays and on Saturdays. In spring, there is a market once a week, on Fridays. In July, Monsieur Banane goes on holiday. He goes to Tunisia, where French is spoken.

1. au mois de mars
2. le vendredi
3. au marché
4. au printemps
5. en été
6. le samedi
7. en juillet
8. en vacances
9. en Tunisie
10. on parle français

Exercice 1.8

Pupils must write a letter in French in which they include certain information. The French for the required information is:

1. il pleut souvent en Angleterre;
2. il fait beau quelquefois;
3. à (...) il y a un cinéma et une piscine;
4. le cinéma est ouvert le vendredi, le samedi et le dimanche;
5. la piscine est toujours ouverte, sauf le jeudi;
6. je vais aller en France en été;
7. je vais rester à Avignon du 8 au 25 août;
8. d'habitude on va en Ecosse pour les grandes vacances;
9. mais cette année c'est différent ...
10. ... parce que ma mère veut manger de la nourriture française!

Exercice 1.9

1. Tu **prends** un coca?
2. Non, je **bois** du café.
3. Nous **buvons** beaucoup d'eau.
4. Ils **prennent** le petit-déjeuner au café.
5. Elle **prend** de la limonade.
6. Je **prends** du jus d'orange.
7. On **boit** du thé en Angleterre.
8. Elles **boivent** du chocolat chaud.
9. Vous **prenez** du sucre?
10. Martin **boit** du sirop de fraise à l'eau.

Exercice 1.10

1. ce crayon
2. cette carte
3. ce livre
4. cette fenêtre
5. ces portes
6. cette règle
7. ce tableau
8. ces chaises
9. cette table
10. ce prof
11. cet ami
12. ces cahiers
13. cet enfant
14. ce stylo
15. cette gomme
16. cette chambre
17. cette cuisine
18. ces pièces
19. ces jardins
20. ce beurre

Exercice 1.11

Pupils must choose any 5 of their answers to Exercice 1.9 and translate them into English. Possible answers are:

1. Are you having a coke?
2. No, I'm drinking coffee.
3. We drink lots of water.
4. They have breakfast in the cafe.
5. She has lemonade.
6. I'm having orange juice.
7. We drink tea in England.
8. They are drinking hot chocolate.
9. Do you take sugar?
10. Martin is drinking strawberry cordial.

Exercice 1.12 - CD: 4

Martine. When is your birthday?
Claire. You forget everything! It's in the spring...
Martine. Oh yes! How silly of me!
Claire. It's on 19th March, like Georges!
Martine. That's right! Sorry!
Georges. And you, Jean-Pierre, when's your birthday?
Jean-Pierre. Mine is 1st August, in summer...
Claire. ...when it's fine and hot!
Martine. Where are you going on holiday?
Jean-Pierre. Usually we go to grandma's house, in les Landes.
Claire. But this year we are going to spend a fortnight in Tunisia!
Georges. Tunisia? Fantastic! You are going to eat couscous..!
Jean-Pierre. Absolutely! We're going to have a good time!
Claire. We are going to go swimming in the warm sea...
Martine. We are going to rent a villa in Bandol.
Claire. That's great! It's lovely down there. Don't forget your camera!

1. She's forgotten when Claire's birthday is.
2. It is on the 19th March.
3. It is fine and hot.
4. They usually go to their grandmother's house in Les Landes.
5. This year they are going to Tunisia.

Exercice 1.13

1. Martine oublie   (d) la date de l'anniversaire de Claire.
2. En Tunisie on   (a) mange du couscous.
3. Claire et Jean-Pierre   (e) vont se baigner.
4. En été il   (c) fait beau et chaud.
5. Le premier août   (b) est en été.

Exercice 1.14

1. Claire oublie son appareil-photo.
2. Martine n'oublie pas l'anniversaire.
3. Martine et Georges vont aller à Bandol.
4. D'habitude on va en Angleterre.
5. Je ne vais pas en Tunisie cette année.
6. En Tunisie ils mangent du couscous.
7. Jean-Pierre veut s'amuser.
8. En été, Claire passe quinze jours en Suisse.
9. Elle veut passer une semaine à Rome.
10. Ils ne vont pas se baigner.
11. Il fait bon mais il pleut.
12. Georges et sa mère prennent du couscous.
13. En Tunisie, en automne, il fait assez bon (c'est assez agréable).
14. Les parents de Claire aiment Lyon quand il ne fait pas trop chaud.
15. Quel temps fait-il à Manchester aujourd'hui?

Exercice 1.15
Two short dialogues
Some friends are on a camping holiday. It is 11pm.

Dialogue 1:

A.	Hey! Are you asleep?
B.	Yes. I'm asleep. What about you?
A.	No. I'm not sleeping. And you are not sleeping! You are lying!
B.	Yes! I'm lying!
A.	Well I'm going out.

Dialogue 2:

C.	Hey! Are you sleeping?
D., E.	Yes, we're sleeping!
C.	But you're lying! You're not sleeping!
D., E.	No! We are not sleeping. We are leaving.
C.	You are leaving?
F.	What are they doing?
G.	They are leaving...
F.	Well I'm sleeping.

Exercice 1.16
In the exercise, pupils write an answer to this letter.

Geneva, 21st June

Dear Anne-Marie,

I am delighted to receive your last letter. Well, it's the holidays soon! I love the holidays. Normally, we go to Italy or Greece, because my parents love the sun and because they are very interested in history. It's quite fun, but my sister and I want to visit the French capital!

So, this year we are going to go to Paris! We are going to rent a flat near the river! We are not going to visit palaces and museums; we are going to go shopping in the department stores, and we are going to eat in restaurants. It's brilliant, isn't it?

Write soon and tell me your holiday plans!

Best wishes,

Joselle

Exercice 1.17

1. Je suis ravie de...
2. Ils s'intéressent beaucoup à l'histoire.
3. C'est assez amusant.
4. On veut visiter la capitale.
5. On va aller à Paris.
6. On va louer.
7. Près de la rivière
8. C'est génial, n'est-ce pas?
9. Ecris-moi vite.
10. Tes projets de vacances.

Exercice 1.18

1. She is in Geneva.
2. They normally go to Italy or Greece.
3. They go there because they are interested in history and they love the sun.
4. They are renting an apartment near the river.
5. They will be shopping, eating in restaurants, and NOT visiting museums and palaces!

Vive la France! Paris

Paris is the capital city of France. It is a big, historic town, very popular with tourists, situated on the banks of the Seine, one of the main rivers of France. There are lots of famous monuments, for example the Eiffel Tower, the Arc de Triomphe and Notre Dame cathedral. But there are also the wide boulevards like the Champs-Elysées, the little streets of the Latin Quarter, and important theatres like the Opéra. The President of the Republic lives and works in Paris.

(b)
1. Paris est la **capitale** de la France.
2. A **Paris**, on peut visiter les **monuments** célèbres.
3. Il y a beaucoup de grands théâtres, comme **l'Opéra**.
4. La rivière qui coule à Paris s'appelle **la Seine.**
5. Le **Président** travaille dans la capitale. Il s'appelle Jacques Chirac*

*Or the name of the current President of France if not Jacques Chirac!

(c) Corrections to the untrue sentences are shown in bold:
1. Le Président habite à **Paris**.
2. L'avenue des Champs Elysées est un **boulevard**.
3. La cathédrale de Paris s'appelle Notre Dame.
4. A Paris on peut visiter beaucoup de musées.
5. La Tour Eiffel est un grand **monument**.

Chapitre 2

After the holidays

Page 16
Picture captions: (left to right)

I'm hungry!   I'm cold!

I'm hot!   I'm thirsty!

Exercice 2.1

j'ai chaud	I'm hot
tu as chaud	you (s.) are hot
il a chaud	he is hot
elle a chaud	she is hot
nous avons chaud	we are hot
vous avez chaud	you (pl.) are hot
ils ont chaud	they (m.) are hot
elles ont chaud	they (f.) are hot

Exercice 2.2

1. Elle a froid.
2. Nous avons faim.
3. J'ai soif.
4. Tu as chaud.
5. Ils ont faim.
6. Il a raison.
7. Vous avez soif.
8. Nous avons tort.
9. Elles ont soif.
10. On a mal.

Exercice 2.3

1. Je n'ai pas faim. — I'm not hungry.
2. Tu n'as pas soif. — You (s.) are not thirsty.
3. Il n'a pas peur. — He's not afraid.
4. Elle n'a pas froid. — She is not cold.
5. Nous n'avons pas soif. — We are not thirsty.
6. Vous n'avez pas mal. — You (pl.) are not in pain.
7. Tu n'as pas chaud. — You (s.) are not hot.
8. Ils n'ont pas froid. — They (m.) are not cold.
9. Vous n'avez pas faim. — You (pl.) are not hungry.
10. Elles n'ont pas tort. — They (f.) are not wrong.
11. Tu n'as pas froid. — You (s.) are not cold.
12. Je n'ai pas froid. — I'm not cold.
13. Elle n'a pas raison. — She is not right.
14. Ils n'ont pas chaud. — They (m.) are not hot.
15. Nous n'avons pas faim. — We are not hungry.

Exercice 2.4 – CD: 5

Dialogue

Georges is in the garden in front of the house. He speaks to the neighbour, M. Simonneau.

M. Simonneau. Hello Georges! How are you?
Georges. Hello M. Simonneau. I'm fine, thanks. And you?
M. Simonneau. I'm all right. Already back from holiday?
Georges. Yes. How about you?
M. Simonneau. No holidays for me! I'm very happy to work in the garden. But you, you're very tanned!
Georges. Ah yes. The sun shone every day in Bandol!
M. Simonneau. I'm sure. What did you do, on holiday?
Georges. Well, I swam in the sea, I went windsurfing, I played football on the beach, I climbed trees, we also had a picnic and we went for walks...
M. Simonneau. Wonderful!

Exercice 2.5

1. J'ai fini.   I have finished *or* I finished.
2. J'ai mangé.   I have eaten *or* I ate.
3. J'ai regardé. I have watched *or* I watched.
4. J'ai trouvé.   I have found *or* I found.
5. J'ai donné.   I have given *or* I gave.

Exercice 2.6

1. Il a fermé.   He has closed *or* he closed.
2. Tu as trouvé.   You (s.) have found *or* you found.
3. Il a mangé.   He has eaten *or* he ate.
4. Elle a rangé.   She has tidied *or* she tidied.
5. Nous avons fini.   We have finished *or* we finished.
6. Vous avez acheté. You (pl.) have bought *or* you bought.
7. Elles ont joué.   They (f.) have played *or* they played.
8. Ils ont gardé.   They (m.) have kept *or* they kept.
9. Tu as marché.   You (s.) have walked *or* you walked.
10. J'ai parlé.   I have spoken *or* I spoke.

Exercice 2.7

Pupils should write a short text in which they use some or all of the following expressions:

1. j'ai regardé   4. j'ai joué
2. j'ai mangé   5. j'ai acheté
3. j'ai nagé

For example:

Lundi, j'ai regardé la télévision à l'hôtel. J'ai nagé dans la mer et j'ai mangé au restaurant. Mardi j'ai acheté un CD. Mercredi j'ai joué avec ma soeur.

Exercice 2.8

1. They (f.) did their homework. / They have done their homework.
2. I have had 4 bananas. / I had 4 bananas.
3. We have been to Morocco.
4. I have read all Simenon's books. / I read all Simenon's books.
5. He wrote to Michèle. / He has written to Michèle.
6. We went windsurfing.
7. You (pl.) have had some coffee. / You had some coffee.
8. Have you (s.) read my letter?
9. They (m.) have been to my house.
10. I wrote a message. / I have written a message.

Exercice 2.9

1. Elle a fait ses devoirs.
2. J'ai eu trois éclairs.
3. Tu as été malade.
4. Nous avons lu le livre.
5. Ils ont écrit à leur tante.
6. Vous avez fait de la planche à voile.
7. Elle a eu une orange.
8. J'ai été en France.
9. On a lu l'avis.
10. Tu as écrit une lettre.

Exercice 2.10 – CD: 6

Dialogue

Georges. I did some drawings as well, and I went fishing!
M. Simonneau. You caught some fish?
Georges. You bet!
M. Simonneau. What about your parents? And Martine?
Georges. My parents played tennis and Martine swam in the campsite swimming pool.
M. Simonneau. Your parents played tennis? So did I, I love tennis!
Georges. And Martine read love stories.
M. Simonneau. That's normal, she's a girl! What did you draw?
Georges. I drew boats. I also drew dad's car.
M. Simonneau. Look. I found this in the garden.
Georges. What is it?
M. Simonneau. It's an old box made of silver.
Georges. Wow!

1. He played football, climbed trees, went for a picnic and for walks, did some drawing and went fishing.
2. Georges's parents played tennis.
3. Martine read love stories and swam in the campsite pool.
4. He thinks it's normal as she is a girl.
5. He found it in the garden.

Exercice 2.11 - CD: 7

Georges spent the summer holidays with all the family in Bandol, a port on the French Riviera. In Bandol, you can go sailing, and there are always a lot of big yachts moored in the marina. But you can do lots of other things too. After the summer holidays, Georges talks to the neighbour, Monsieur Simonneau. M. Simonneau asks Georges, "What did you do on holiday?" Georges did lots of things. He went windsurfing, he swam in the sea, he played football on the beach, he caught fish, and he drew. Georges draws well. His sister Martine read romantic comic books. Suddenly, M. Simonneau shows Georges a little silver box. He has found the box in his garden. It is very old, and very dirty. It is black! Georges looks at the box.

1. It's a Mediterranean resort with a marina.
2. It is on the Côte d'Azur (traditionally known as the French Riviera in English).
3. The box is black with dirt, even though it is made of silver.

Exercice 2.12

(Note to teachers. The first printing of the Pupil's book contains an error instructing pupils to use Exercice 2.10 to find 10 verbs in the present; however, this should say use Exercice 2.11, and the following examples are taken from Exercice 2.11.)

Verbs in the present: Verbs in the passé composé:

1. on peut   1. Georges a passé
2. (il y) a   2. tu as fait
3. on peut   3. il a fait
4. parle   4. il a fait
5. demande   5. il a nagé
6. dessine   6. il a joué
7. montre   7. il a pêché
8. est   8. il a dessiné
9. est   9. Martine a lu
10. regarde   10. il a trouvé

Exercice 2.13

| NAGER | VOILE | MER | VACANCES | DESSINER |
| POISSON | BOITE | ARGENT | PORT | PLANCHE |

Exercice 2.14

1. Georges **a** passé les grandes vacances à Bandol. Georges spent his summer holiday in Bandol.
2. Il **a** fait beaucoup de choses. He has done lots of things.
3. Martine **a** lu des bandes dessinées. Martine has read comics.
4. M. Simonneau et Georges **ont** discuté. M. Simmoneau and Georges had a chat.
5. Les parents de Georges **ont** joué au tennis. Georges' parents played tennis.
6. J'**ai** trouvé une boîte. I have found a box.
7. Vous **avez** passé deux semaines en Egypte? Did you spend two weeks in Egypt?
8. Oui, nous **avons** visité les Pyramides. Yes, we visited the Pyramids.
9. Martine **a** fait de la voile? Did Martine go sailing?
10. Non, mais elle **a** dessiné. No, but she drew.

Exercice 2.15

1. Georges **a parlé** à M. Simonneau.
2. Nathalie et Jean-Luc **ont discuté** pendant la pause.
3. Marie-Claire **a écouté** la radio.
4. Maman **a chanté** ce matin.
5. Papa et Martine **ont été** à Paris.
6. J'ai fait mes devoirs, et j'**ai regardé** la télévision.
7. Georges et Nicole **ont pêché** des poissons.
8. Vous **avez écouté** les informations?
9. J'**ai été** malade.

Exercice 2.16

1. Georges spoke to M. Simonneau.
2. Nathalie and Jean-Luc chatted during the break.
3. Marie-Claire listened to the radio.
4. Mum sang this morning.
5. Papa and Martine have been to Paris.
6. I did my homework and I watched television.
7. Georges and Nicole caught some fish.
8. Did you listen to the news?
9. I was ill. / I have been ill.

Exercice 2.17

Chanter

j'ai chanté	nous avons chanté
tu as chanté	vous avez chanté
il a chanté	ils ont chanté
elle a chanté	elles ont chanté

Choisir

j'ai choisi	nous avons choisi
tu as choisi	vous avez choisi
il a choisi	ils ont choisi
elle a choisi	elles ont choisi

Vendre

j'ai vendu	nous avons vendu
tu as vendu	vous avez vendu
il a vendu	ils ont vendu
elle a vendu	elles ont vendu

Exercice 2.18

> (e.g.) Oxford, le 21 septembre
>
> Cher.......... / Chère ....,
>
> Ça va? Moi, ça va bien. J'ai été en vacances. J'ai nagé dans la piscine de l'hôtel et j'ai fait de la planche à voile. Mon frère a pêché (ou: a attrapé) des poissons. J'ai joué au football sur la plage et mes soeurs ont acheté de beaux vêtements.
>
> Ecris-moi bientôt
>
> Amicalement (best wishes)   /   Gros bisous (love from)
>
> ....

Vive la France!

Books of comic strips are extremely popular in France, not only among children but also with adults. There are lots of comics for the young and for grown-ups: romantic or funny stories, historical adventures, traditional tales. 'French' comic strips are known the world over, especially Tintin and Asterix. But there's a surprise! Did you know that Tintin is Belgian? His creator is called Hergé (pronounced like the French names for the letters R and G – the reversed initials of his real name Georges, Rémi) and he comes from Brussels.

(b)   TINTIN   HERGE   BANDES   DESSINEES   CONTES

   ASTERIX   BELGE   REMI   COMIQUE   BRUXELLES

(c)   Pupils copy any five French words from the passage in mirror-writing for their partner to decipher. The partner must also pronounce the words and say what they mean.

Chapitre 3

The Silver Box

Exercice 3.1 - CD: 8

Dialogue

M. Simonneau and Georges are still chatting about the silver box.

M. Simonneau. It's very old...
Georges. It certainly is. I'm going to open the box. Look, there is something...
M. Simonneau. What do you see?
Georges. I see some initials. Wait... er: well, I don't know. It's too dirty!
M. Simonneau. I can clean the box, if you want.

M. Simonneau cleans the box with a special cleaning fluid in his garage.

M. Simonneau. There! We can see really clearly now!
Georges. Show me! Oh yes! "J-P. L." – But who is it?
M. Simonneau. I don't know. Do you know a Jean-Pierre? A Jean-Paul?
Georges. Yes, but the box is old. It's not my friend Jean-Pierre's.
M. Simonneau. No. We must think. Perhaps it belongs to another person who has lived in this house.
Georges. But what are we going to do to discover who it is?

Exercice 3.2 - CD: 9

Pupils are trained to recite the French alphabet correctly.

The best way is in the groups of letters indicated in the pupils' book. The CD should be used.

Exercice 3.3 - CD: 10

Spelling aloud in French.

The questions are asked by one pupil to another, after appropriate examples have been given. Below are the meanings of the questions asked:

1. What is your name? How do you spell it?
2. What is her name? How do you spell it?
3. What is it? How do you spell it?
4. What is that called? How does one spell violon ?

Exercice 3.4

1. La boîte est petite, vieille et sale.
2. Sur la boîte, il voit des initiales.
3. M. Simonneau nettoie la boîte, avec un produit spécial.
4. Il nettoie la boîte parce qu'elle est sale.

Exercice 3.5

1. Georges **ouvre** la fenêtre de la cuisine.
2. Marie-Claire **ferme** la porte du salon.
3. Pourquoi n'**ouvres**-tu pas la fenêtre?
4. Parce qu'il **fait** froid.
5. **A**-t-il fini son livre?
6. Non, il **lit** en ce moment.
7. Est-ce qu'il **ouvre** sa trousse?
8. On ne **suit** pas.
9. Ils **ouvrent** le magasin à neuf heures.
10. Vous **suivez** les directions.

Exercice 3.6

1. **Elle*** suit son père à la plage.
2. A Noël, **nous** ouvrons les cadeaux.
3. **Tu** veux un croissant, chérie?
4. Oui **je** veux bien, Papa.
5. **Elle*** suit la route de Nîmes.
6. **Ils*** ouvrent la boîte.
7. D'habitude, **nous** suivons les instructions.
8. **Vous** ouvrez à quelle heure, s'il vous plaît?
9. **Ils*** veulent entrer dans le café.
10. **Tu** es français, ou belge?

*Depending on the context, il, elle and on are interchangeable in exercises like this one, since they have the same verb forms. The same is true for ils and elles.

Exercice 3.7

1. Il n'a pas trouvé.
2. Nous n'avons pas écouté.
3. Vous n'avez pas continué.
4. On n'a pas écrit.
5. Tu n'as pas lu.
6. Ils n'ont pas parlé.
7. Je n'ai pas mangé.
8. Philippe n'a pas entendu.
9. Maman n'a pas chanté.
10. Jacques et Martine n'ont pas regardé.

Exercice 3.8

1. Georges **a vu** des initiales dans la boîte.
2. Martine **a bu** de la limonade.
3. Maman **a couru** à la banque.
4. La banque **a fermé** a midi vingt.
5. Le professeur **a dit** "au revoir" à Madame Dupont.
6. Tu **n'as pas mis** ton pull?
7. Je **n'ai pas pu**. Il est à l'école.
8. M. Simonneau **n'a pas voulu** une tasse de café.
9. Marcel **n'a pas ouvert** la porte.
10. Papa **n'a pas pris** de pain.

Exercice 3.9

1. Je **dîne** chez Jean-Pierre.
2. Tu **finis** mon livre aujourd'hui?
3. Je **cours** chez le marchand de journaux.
4. Vous **mangez** bien à l'école?
5. Tu **rends** ton cahier de géographie.
6. Il **a** trois croissants!
7. On **mange** à treize heures.
8. Papa et maman **attendent** à l'arrêt de bus.
9. Vous **êtes** au restaurant.
10. Nous **visitons** le château.

Exercice 3.10

1. Georges **sait** ouvrir la boîte.
2. M. Simonneau **connaît** la maison.
3. Vous **savez** nager?
4. Non, je ne **sais** pas nager.
5. Martine **connaît** mon ami Jules.
6. Nous **savons** écrire en français.
7. **Peux**-tu lire ce livre anglais?
8. On **connaît** les chants de Noël.
9. Philippe et Marcel **savent** faire du VTT.
10. **Connaissez**-vous la famille Durand?

Exercice 3.11 – CD: 11

Dialogue

M. Simonneau. Ah, the coffee is so good.
Papa. So, Paul. Your garden's all right?
M. Simonneau. Oh yes. We've had some good weather this year. Where did you go on holiday?
Maman. We went to Bandol, on the Riviera. The weather was good, really good. The sun shone every day!
Martine. Every day except one, mum. The Wednesday when we went to the cinema?
Maman. Oh yes! It rained all day and we decided to go to the cinema.
Papa. And everyone had the same idea as us!
Georges. Martine went to pay and we went into the cinema, but we didn't find any seats!
Martine. And afterwards, we went to the restaurant. What a fiasco it was!
M. Simonneau. Why?
Papa. Because Georges and I chose the set menu straight away.
Georges. But mum and Martine couldn't make up their minds! Can you magine...

Exercice 3.12

Note: the examples in this exercise were meant to be translated into French, not English, as stated in the Pupil's Book!

1. Il est monté.
2. John est arrivé.
3. Philippe est venu.
4. Je suis entré(e)*.
5. Tu es resté(e)*.
6. Il est descendu.
7. Je suis tombé(e)*.
8. Tu es né(e)*.
9. Il est parti.
10. Tu es sorti(e).

*Je and tu, as well as nous and vous, may of course be either masculine or feminine.

Exercice 3.13

1. Il **est** allé au théâtre.
2. Elle **est** arrivée à la piscine.
3. Nous **sommes** partis de la maison.
4. Tu **es** rentré à quelle heure?
5. Ils **sont** tombés de l'arbre.
6. Vous **êtes** venus de quelle direction?
7. Elles **sont** entrées dans la salle.
8. Je **suis** monté par l'escalier.
9. Marie **est** retournée à trois heures.
10. Jean et Philippe **sont** descendus à midi.

Exercice 3.14

1. Nous sommes part**is** de Paris hier.
2. Tu es sort**ie** après le déjeuner, Marie?
3. Pierre est rentré tout de suite après les cours.
4. Georges et Martine sont venu**s** à la maison.
5. Pauline est descendu**e** de sa chambre quand le courrier est arrivé.
6. Jean et moi, on est arrivé**s** à la gare à 15 h.
7. Vous êtes allé**e** à la boulangerie, madame?
8. Tu es tombé, Christophe?
9. Georges et Jacques sont retourné**s** à la maison.
10. Martine et Sophie sont resté**es** dans les magasins.

Exercice 3.15

	verbe	anglais	participe passé	auxiliaire
1.	acheter	to buy	acheté	avoir
2.	aimer	to like	aimé	avoir
3.	aller	to go	allé	être
4.	arriver	to arrive	arrivé	être
5.	boire	to drink	bu	avoir
6.	connaître	to know	connu	avoir
7.	devoir	to have to (must)	dû	avoir
8.	dire	to say	dit	avoir
9.	lire	to read	lu	avoir
10.	mettre	to put (on)	mis	avoir
11.	mourir	to die	mort	être
12.	nettoyer	to clean	nettoyé	avoir
13.	payer	to pay (for)	payé	avoir
14.	pouvoir	to be able	pu	avoir
15.	prendre	to take	pris	avoir
16.	rester	to stay	resté	être
17.	savoir	to know	su	avoir
18.	tomber	to fall	tombé	être
19.	venir	to come	venu	être
20.	vouloir	to want	voulu	avoir

Exercice 3.16

1. Nous avons aimé le film.
2. Après le déjeuner, vous êtes arrivé(e)(s) au centre-ville.
3. Tu as bu de la bière hier soir?
4. Ils ont pensé que je m'appelle Cédric!
5. Nous avons dû traverser la rue.
6. Jeudi dernier, je suis resté(e) chez moi.
7. On a dit des bêtises.
8. Tu n'as pas voulu manger le steak?
9. Elle est morte mercredi matin.
10. J'ai payé le médicament.

Exercice 3.17

1. They have not been able to (were not able to; could not) go to the cinema.
2. Joselle has put (put) her books on the table.
3. Have you not read his (her) name?
4. I knew Philippe in Lyon.
5. Mum and dad have tidied the garage.
6. Marion fell outside (in front of) the house.
7. She did not stay: she left.
8. To go to school, I took the bus.
9. Georges bought a CD for Martine.
10. She (has) listened to the disc.

Exercice 3.18 – CD: 12

Passage and dialogue.

Dad, mum, Martine and Georges are in the Trois Caves restaurant. There are set menus at 15, 20 and 28 euros. Georges and his dad look at the 15 euro menu and decide straight away, but Martine and her mum are not sure. Dad chooses the trout, and Georges chooses a steak. Mum decides to have the salmon but Martine prefers the chicken with rice.

(The waiter arrives.)

Waiter. Good evening. Are you ready to order? (*literally*, have you chosen?)
Dad. Good evening. The 15 euro menu for everyone, please. I'm going to have the trout meunière.
Georges. Can I have the steak and chips, dad?
Dad. Of course. Right. What are you having, darling?
Mum. Mmm. I don't know. The salmon, perhaps.
Martine. I'd like the chicken and rice.
Waiter. Right. One trout, one steak, one chicken with rice, one salmon...
Mum. No! Hang on! I'm changing my mind. I'll have the chicken as well.
Waiter. Right. Two chicken with rice...
Martine. No! I'd like a steak, like Georges.
Waiter. So. One trout, two steaks, one chicken with rice. Is that right?
Dad. Er... yes. At least, I think so!

Answers to the questions below the vocabulary:
1. There are three set menus.
2. He decides that they will choose from the 15 euro menu.
3. Her first choice is salmon.
4. One person has chicken in the end.
5. The English for the restaurant name is "The Three Cellars".

Exercice 3.19

1. Vous avez choisi?
2. Je vais prendre...
3. Je peux avoir...?
4. Qu'est-ce que tu prends?
5. Je voudrais le poulet.
6. Non! Attendez...

Exercice 3.20

Pupils have to write in full one of the verbs **payer, envoyer, essayer** or **essuyer**.

The important thing is that the spellings of the verb stems are different for pronounced and unpronounced endings:

Payer	**Other verbs**		
je paie	j'envoie	j'essaie	j'essuie
tu paies	tu envoies	tu essaies	tu essuies
il paie	il envoie	il essaie	il essuie
elle paie	elle envoie	elle essaie	elle essuie
nous payons	**nous envoyons**	**nous essayons**	**nous essuyons**
vous payez	**vous envoyez**	**vous essayez**	**vous essuyez**
ils paient	ils envoient	ils essaient	ils essuient
elles paient	elles envoient	elles essaient	elles essuient

Vive la France!

(a) Lots of French families go on holiday in the mountains, in the Alps or the Pyrenees, near the Swiss, Italian and Spanish borders, in winter or in spring. One can do all sorts of activities: skiing, tobogganing, skating, and, of course, eating the mountain food specialities which are delicious! On the snow-covered slopes, or at the ice-rinks, you meet lots of foreigners: English, Germans, Italians, Dutch... In the Alps there are some very famous ski resorts: Chamonix-Mont-Blanc, Albertville, Val d'Isère, Tignes, Les Gets.

(b) 1. Tania est allée en France.
    2. Marcel est allé en Italie.
    3. Anne est allée à Albertville.
    4. Philippe est allé à Tignes.
    5. Sophie est allée à Val d'Isère.

(c) 1. près des frontières.
    2. faire de la luge.
    3. les spécialités de la montagne.
    4. on rencontre beaucoup d'étrangers.
    5. des stations de ski.

Chapitre 4

Where shall we eat this evening?

Exercice 4.1 – CD: 13

Dialogue

The following day, M. Simonneau and Georges continued their conversation in the garden.

M. Simonneau. You had nice food on holiday, did you?
Georges. Oh yes. On the 'Wednesday of the cinema' we ate really well.
M. Simonneau. What did you have?
Georges. I had the steak and chips. But we went to other restaurants, too.
M. Simonneau. Oh yes? Tell me all!
Georges. Right. First, we went to a fish restaurant next to the beach. It was unfortunate because Martine doesn't like fish.
M. Simonneau. Ah. Still, not everyone likes fish...
Georges. We looked at the set-price menus and the full menu. She chose a herb omelette, eventually! Then one day we had dinner in an Italian restaurant. It was really great.
M. Simonneau. Me, I like pasta and pizzas.
Georges. Me too! Afterwards, the Friday lunchtime, mum wanted to try some sea food, so we booked a table in a little restaurant where we had mussels. It was excellent.
M. Simonneau. Stop! You're making me hungry (literally: you give me hunger)!

Pupils are asked to work in pairs reading the dialogue.

Exercice 4.2

1. Qu'est-ce que tu as pris?
2. On est allés dans d'autres restaurants.
3. Tout le monde n'aime pas le poisson.
4. On a dîné.
5. On a réservé une table.
6. Vendredi midi.
7. Elle a choisi une omelette.

Exercice 4.3

1. Qu'est-ce qu'elle a pris?
2. On est allés à d'autres villes.
3. Tout le monde n'écrit pas avec un stylo.
4. Ils ont déjeuné.
5. Papa a réservé une chambre à l'hôtel.
6. Mercredi matin.
7. J'ai décidé de prendre le steak.

Exercice 4.4 – CD: 14

Dialogue

We are at the Chez Nadia restaurant. Tochiko and her friends come in.

Tochiko. Cool! I love this restaurant.
Alice. So do I. And eating here isn't expensive!
Joséphine. That's true. Excuse me! Can we find a place to sit?
Waiter Of course! How many are you?

Joséphine. There are three of us.
Waiter No problem. Wherever you want!
Tochiko. Where shall we go?
Alice. There, near the window. It's nice and you can see everything.
Tochiko. OK.
Waiter. I'll bring the menu, girls!
Tochiko. Thank you!

Exercice 4.5 – CD: 15

(The French original is a pronunciation practice task.)

Chez Nadia is an Algerian restaurant. In France there are many foreign restaurants. Nadia is a friend of Christine, Tochiko's mother. She does the cooking in her restaurant. Tochiko loves Algerian cooking. On Friday evening, she went to Chez Nadia with her two friends Alice and Joséphine. The waiter brought the menu. The menu was very attractive and very long! Tochiko looked at the starters, the main courses and the desserts. She could not choose! She asked her friends, "What have you chosen?" Joséphine answered first:

"I'm going to have the couscous with chicken and vegetables."
"Me, I'd like a rice salad with beans," said Alice.
"Aren't you hungry?" asked Tochiko.
"Yes! But I would like couscous afterwards!"
"OK. What are we having to drink?"
"Some water and... coca cola."

Exercice 4.6

1. It is an Algerian restaurant.
2. Nadia herself does the cooking.
3. She is a friend of Tochiko's mother.
4. She went there on Friday evening.
5. She went with her friends Alice and Joséphine.
6. The menu was very varied and attractive.
7. Because she could not make up her mind.
8. They had water and coca cola.

Exercice 4.7

Pupils make up a menu. The dishes should come under the headings below as follows:

1. **Nos entrées**
   salade de riz avec haricots
   champignons à l'ail
   taboulé

2. **Nos plats principaux**
   brochette d'agneau
   couscous au poulet et aux légumes
   omelette au fromage ou aux champignons

3. **Nos fromages**
   fromage de chèvre
   camembert

4. **Nos desserts**
   coupe spéciale Nadia
   sorbet au citron
   glaces (une, deux ou trois boules)
   salade de fruits

5. **Nos boissons**
   coca cola
   eau minérale gazeuse
   thé à la menthe
   vin rouge ou blanc en pichet

Exercice 4.8 - CD: 16

Dialogue

M. Simonneau. Hi! So, on holiday you discovered the restaurants of Bandol.
Dad. That's right. But we also had a picnic in the countryside.
M. Simonneau. A picnic! Eating in the open air! Making the most of nature, the sun, the birds singing in the trees...
Dad. ...the mosquitos!
M. Simonneau. Well, yes. So, what did you have to eat?
Dad. My wife bought some bread, butter and cheese, and Martine and Georges went to the charcuterie.
M. Simonneau. And what did they find?
Dad. Let me think... some salads, like Russian salad, grated carrots, celery salad, tomatoes and, of course, ham, salami and pâté.
M. Simonneau. Well done kids! And what did you drink?
Dad. Local wine, water, and Orangina for the children.

Pupils are asked to prepare and present this dialogue in front of the class.

Exercice 4.9

1. He thinks they are wonderful.
2. He mentions the mosquitos.
3. Mum bought the cheese.
4. They bought the picnic ingredients at the charcuterie (delicatessen).
5. The grown-ups had local wine and water and the children had Orangina.

Exercice 4.10

1. Georges et Martine ont acheté de la viande froide.
2. M. Simonneau a parlé au papa de Georges.
3. Martine a choisi du céléri.
4. Ils sont allés à la campagne.
5. Elle est allée à la plage.
6. Nous sommes entré(e)s dans la charcuterie.
7. Tu as lu ton livre de bandes dessinées.
8. Maman a voulu du vin de pays.
9. Papa n'a pas pu trouver le restaurant.
10. Martine est sortie de la maison.

Exercice 4.11

1. Est-ce que tu as acheté trois kilos de tomates?
2. Marie et Julien sont sortis à huit heures.
3. Maman a parlé au boulanger ce matin.
4. Je n'ai pas pu trouver le chat de ma grand-mère.
5. N'as-tu pas choisi une robe pour ce soir?
6. Marcel n'a pas voulu entrer dans le magasin.
7. As-tu lu le dernier roman de Troyat?
8. Nous sommes allés à Biarritz l'année dernière.

9. Le chien est entré dans la maison.
10. Elle n'est pas descendue de la voiture.
11. Ils sont montés dans le bus.
12. Le prof a puni notre ami(e).
13. Elle n'a pas pu trouver l'adresse.
14. Claude et Nicolas sont revenus (or: retournés or: rentrés) ce matin.
15. Pauline a vu le film.

Exercice 4.12

Pupils choose one verb from the list and write it out in full:

je me suis trouvé(e)   nous nous sommes trouvé(e)s
tu t'es trouvé(e)   vous vous êtes trouvé(e)(s)
il s'est trouvé   ils se sont trouvés
elle s'est trouvée   elles se sont trouvées

je me suis arrêté(e)   nous nous sommes arrêté(e)s
tu t'es arrêté(e)   vous vous êtes arrêté (e)(s)
il s'est arrêté   ils se sont arrêtés
elle s'est arrêtée   elles se sont arrêtées

je me suis disputé(e)   nous nous sommes disputé(e)s
tu t'es disputé(e)   vous vous êtes disputé(e)(s)
il s'est disputé   ils se sont disputés
elle s'est disputée   elles se sont disputées

je me suis reposé(e)   nous nous sommes reposé(e)s
tu t'es reposé(e)   vous vous êtes reposé(e)(s)
il s'est reposé   ils se sont reposés
elle s'est reposée   elles se sont reposées

je me suis rappelé(e)   nous nous sommes rappelé(e)s
tu t'es rappelé(e)   vous vous êtes rappelé(e)(s)
il s'est rappelé   ils se sont rappelés
elle s'est rappelée   elles se sont rappelées

je me suis baigné(e)   nous nous sommes baigné(e)s
tu t'es baigné(e)   vous vous êtes baigné(e)(s)
il s'est baigné   ils se sont baignés
elle s'est baignée   elles se sont baignées

Exercice 4.13

1. I stopped at the swimming pool.
2. She argued with her brother.
3. We rested after lunch.
4. You found yourself in the town centre.
5. He argued with me.
6. The bus stopped outside the cinema.

7. Mum rested before the film.
8. Pierre found himself on the beach.
9. Christine's car stopped.
10. I got up at six o'clock this morning!
11. Claire did not get up for breakfast.
12. They did not argue.
13. Papa did not rest this evening.
14. Tochiko and Martine did not bathe in the river.
15. They found themselves in Paris.

Exercice 4.14

The correct versions of the sentences are:

1. Maman s'est lavée ce matin.
2. Pierre s'est arrêté aux feux.
3. Je me suis reposé dans le salon.
4. Nous nous sommes regardés (regardées – all f.) dans la glace.
5. Vous vous êtes installés (installées – all f.) à table.

The Silver Box (2) – CD: 17

It is the evening. The whole family has eaten and left the table. They are relaxing in the sitting room.

Georges.   Dad, M. Simonneau has cleaned the box.
Papa   Which box?
Georges.   The little silver box. Look. There are initials.
Papa.   Let's see. J-P. L. Who is it?
Georges.   I don't know.
Papa.   Perhaps it is a former inhabitant of the village.
Georges.   Or of M. Simonneau's house?
Papa.   You can show it to mummy.
Georges.   Why?
Papa.   She's interested in antiques.
Georges.   Mum, are you asleep?
Mum.   Oh! goodness! I fell asleep!
Georges.   Are you awake now?
Mum.   Of course, dear. What's the matter?
Georges.   The silver box. Look!
Mum.   It is beautiful.
Georges.   There are some initials.
Mum.   Yes, I see them. J-P.L. Jean-Paul? Jean-Pierre?
Papa.   We should speak to Grandma.
Mum.   Good idea!

Exercice 4.15

1. Maman **les** voit. Mum sees them.
2. Georges **la** montre à maman. Georges shows it to mum.
3. Papa **les** regarde. Dad looks at them.
4. Christine **le** veut. Christine wants it.
5. Martine et papa **le** mangent. Martine and dad eat it.
6. M. Simonneau **la** trouve. M. Simmoneau finds it.
7. Le prof **le** lit. The teacher reads it.
8. Les enfants **l'**écoutent. The children listen to him.
9. Marie-Claire **le** quitte. Marie-Claire leaves him.
10. Zazie **les** aime. Zazie likes them.

Exercice 4.16

1. Paul et Philippe **le** regardent.
2. Jacqueline **la** nettoie.
3. Claire **l'**aime.
4. Pauline **les** préfère.
5. Moi je **les** adore.
6. Maman **la** commande.
7. Pierre **l'**écoute.
8. Le prof **la** raconte.
9. Tu **le** veux?
10. Oui, je **le** veux.

Exercice 4.17

The answers, using pronouns, for B:
1. Oui, je le vois.
2. Oui, je la mange.
3. Oui, je le regarde.
4. Oui, je les aime.
5. Oui, je la touche.
6. Oui, je la range.
7. Oui, je les aide.
8. Oui, je le trouve.
9. Oui, je la préfère.
10. Oui, je la déteste.

Vive la France

People often speak about the historical monuments in France. But there are also buildings which are good examples of modern architecture and creativity. In Paris, in front of the Louvre, a very old building, there is a glass pyramid (finished in 1988) which houses the underground part of the museum. In Poitiers, a town situated in the mid-west of the country, there is a theme park called Futuroscope, opened to the public in 1987, which is devoted to the very latest audio-visual techniques. The architecture of certain buildings is stunning.

(b)
1. Le musée est un bâtiment moderne.
2. Quand j'ai visité Paris j'ai vu des bâtiments étonnants.
3. Il y a une pyramide de verre devant le musée.
4. Futuroscope à Poitiers est un parc d'attractions.
5. En France on trouve beaucoup d'exemples de créativité.

Chapitre 5

At the doctor's

Exercice 5.1 – CD: 18

Dialogue

M. Simonneau. Ouch! That hurts! I must go to the doctor's.
Dad. What's wrong?
M. Simonneau. I have a bad back. It's probably the gardening.
Dad. By the way, Georges went to hospital on holiday.
M. Simonneau. Really? Why?
Dad. He fell off his bicycle. I phoned the hospital, and we set off straight away.
M. Simonneau. He didn't say anything.
Dad. It isn't serious. It's fine now.

(Georges comes outside)

Georges. Hello Mr. Simonneau.
M. Simonneau. Hi Georges. So, you fell off your bike?
Georges. Yes, but it's nothing. I hurt myself, that's all. I was lucky.
M. Simonneau. Why?
Georges. I have a friend who fell from a horse. He broke his arm!
M. Simonneau. Oh dear! Listen, Do you still have the silver box?
Georges. Of course. We are going to show it to Grandma. She has lived here all her life.

Exercice 5.2

1. He has a bad back.
2. He hurt his back doing the gardening.
3. He is going to go to the doctor's.
4. Georges fell off his bicycle on holiday.
5. He considers himself lucky because a friend of his fell from a horse and broke his arm.

Exercice 5.3

1. J'ai mal à la main.
2. Tu as mal à l'épaule.
3. Il a mal aux jambes.
4. Vous avez mal au bras?
5. J'ai mal au ventre.
6. Elle a mal à la tête.
7. Tu as mal à la gorge?
8. Non, j'ai mal aux dents.
9. M. Duval a mal au nez.
10. Valérie a mal au cou.
11. J'ai mal au coude.
12. On a mal aux épaules.
13. Tu as mal à la tête?
14. Il a mal au genou.
15. Elle a mal au ventre.

Exercice 5.4 CD: 19

M. Simonneau makes an appointment.
(M. Simonneau dials the doctor's telephone number.)

Receptionist. Hello. Doctor Flaubert's surgery.
M. Simonneau. Ah yes. Good morning. I'd like to make an appointment to see Doctor Flaubert.
Receptionist. Yes sir. You are Mr. ...?
M. Simonneau. Simonneau. S I M O N N E A U.
Receptionist. Which day would you like to come?
M. Simonneau. Tomorrow, please. Tomorrow if possible at around 11 o'clock.
Receptionist. Fine. Tomorrow, Tuesday, at ... 10.45? Is that OK?
M. Simonneau. That's perfect.
Receptionist. Right. See you on Monday 5th September. It's in the diary!
M. Simonneau. Thank you madam. Goodbye.
Receptionist. Thank you sir. See you tomorrow. Goodbye.

Exercice 5.5 - CD: 20

Dialogue

In Doctor Flaubert's surgery.

Receptionist. M. Simonneau?
M. Simonneau. That's me, yes.
Receptionist. Follow me please.
Dr. Flaubert. Good morning M. Simonneau. Now, what seems to be the trouble?
M. Simonneau. It's my back, doctor. My back hurts.
Dr. Flaubert. I see. Lie down there. We'll have a look at it. Does that hurt... there?
M. Simonneau. No...
Dr. Flaubert. And ...there?
M. Simonneau. Ow! Yes! That really hurts!
Dr. Flaubert. Do you do any gardening?
M. Simonneau. Yes. This week, I've done a lot of gardening.
Dr. Flaubert. I'm not surprised. I'm going to give you a prescription. Go to Maurice the Chemist's in the rue des Saules. Buy this cream. Put some cream on your back, twice a day.
M. Simonneau. Thank you, doctor. Goodbye.
Dr. Flaubert. Goodbye sir.

Exercice 5.6

1. Ouvre la boîte!
2. Partez à dix heures!
3. Cherche ton cahier!
4. Rentrons à la maison!
5. Ferme la porte!
6. Lisez le texte!
7. Ecris à ta tante!
8. Sortons d'ici!
9. Parle à Mamie!
10. Soyez sages, les enfants!

Exercice 5.7

1. Ouvre la porte!
2. ferme la fenêtre!
3. Touche le plafond / le plancher!
4. Ecris ton nom au tableau!
5. Donne ta trousse!
6. Allonge-toi par terre!
7. Lève-toi!
8. Mets-toi devant la porte!
9. Couche-toi!
10. Assieds-toi!

The Silver Box (continued) CD: 21

It's the following day. Martine and Georges have left the house to go to their grandmother's.

Georges. When was the last time we saw granny?
Martine. I don't know. Before the holidays.
Georges. You're right. She's going to say...
Martine. ...that we never come!
Georges. Yes! But it's no joke, at her age.
Martine. No. She's eighty-five: she has trouble going out.
Georges. She never goes out, she sees no-one, she does nothing.
Martine. Oh yes she does! She does her cooking, she reads, she writes letters...

Exercice 5.8 CD: 22

Dialogue
The children arrive at their granny's house.

(Martine rings the doorbell, and Georges knocks gently on the door)

Georges. I hear nothing. She is not there.
Martine. Yes she is. Wait a bit.

Suddenly there is a creak. The door opens.

Mamie. Ah! There you are! Daddy phoned me. Come in! Come into the kitchen!
Martine. Hello Mamie! Are you well?
Mamie. I'm all right, but my arms and my left hand hurt.
Georges. Your left hand?
Mamie. Yes. The doctor has told me that I write too many letters! Do you want some coca cola?
Martine. Yes please. You went to the doctor's?
Mamie. Of course not! He comes here. I have difficulty walking, you know.
Georges. Yes, I know. Does he come every day?
Mamie. No, not every day. He comes every week.
Martine. Georges wants to ask you something.
Mamie. Really? Well my dear, I'm listening!
Georges. You know, M. Simonneau found treasure in his garden.
Mamie. Oh yes? What treasure?
Georges. A little silver box. Look.

1. They last saw her before the holidays.
2. She is 85.
3. She never goes out.
4. She cooks, reads and writes letters.
5. She knows because their father phoned to tell her.
6. She has bad arms and her left hand hurts.
7. She writes with her left hand.

Exercice 5.9 – CD: 23

Georges begins to tell the story of the silver box. He tells granny that M. Simonneau has found the box but that they do not know the identity of its owner. He shows the box to granny, who takes her old glasses and puts them on her nose. She looks at the initials J-P. L. She does not recognise them. But suddenly, she stops. She raises her eyes, looks straight ahead of her and says, in a mysterious voice, *I wonder...* Granny gets up and goes into the dining room, where she begins to flip through an old photo album. Martine drinks her cola in silence. She looks at her brother. Georges looks at the box.

1.	Martine tells the story of the box to granny.	Faux	False
2.	Mamie finds it hard to see and to read.	Faux	False
3.	She does not know the identity of J-P.L.	Vrai	True
4.	Mamie leaves the kitchen.	Vrai	True

Exercice 5.10

1. Georges a commencé à raconter l'histoire.
2. Il a dit que Martine boit du coca.
3. Georges a montré la boîte à Mamie.
4. Mamie a pris ses lunettes.
5. Soudain, elle s'est arrêtée.
6. Elle a regardé les initiales.
7. La grand-mère s'est levée.
8. Je me suis demandé.
9. Martine a bu son coca.
10. Georges s'est demandé.

Exercice 5.11

(1. jambe   jambe = leg   *the others are fruits; given as an example*)
2. pomme   pomme = apple   the others are all classroom equipment.
c'est un fruit.
3. voile   voile = sailing   the others are all items of clothing.
c'est un sport.
4. brun   brun = brown   the others are all parts of the body.
c'est une couleur.
5. gomme   gomme = eraser   the others are all sports.
c'est un article de classe.
6. bras   bras = arm   the others are all colours.
c'est une partie du corps.

Exercice 5.12

Pupils should write a letter in answer to the one they are supposed to have 'received' from Pierrette in the exercise. They are asked to include the following things, which are numbered here for ease of marking:

Town, then date in French

Chère Pierrette,

(...)

1. Lundi, j'ai été malade.
2. Hier je suis allé(e) chez le médecin, qui m'a donné une ordonnance.
3. Je suis allé (e) à la pharmacie.
4. J'ai acheté des comprimés et du sirop.
5. Aujourd'hui à Nice, il fait beau.
6. Je vais jouer au tennis.

There should follow a standard ending to a letter in French, e.g:

Amicalement,   (name)

Exercice 5.13 - CD: 24

Dialogue

Tochiko goes to the pharmacy (chemist's) in town. She must make some purchases for all the family.

(She goes into the shop.)

Chemist. Good morning, young lady. How are you?
Tochiko. Good morning. I'm fine thank you. But I'm hot!
Chemist. Yes. It is hot today. But it's the end of the summer. So...
Tochiko. So. Today, I need... wait. I have a list.
Chemist. I'm listening (to you)!
Tochiko. I'd like: some toothpaste for Marie-Christine, a tooth brush for mum, pastilles for Pascal, Mina wants some shampoo, and for me some soap and a comb. And then, grandfather's pills, please.
Chemist. Do you have the prescription?
Tochiko. Yes! Here it is. Here...

1. She's feeling fine.
2. It is the end of the summer.
3. Tochiko has a list.
4. She needs a prescription.
5. For herself, she wants some soap and a comb.

Exercice 5.14

Tochiko est allée à la pharmacie en ville aujourd'hui avec une liste. Elle a acheté beaucoup de choses: du dentifrice, un peigne, du shampooing et des pastilles. Moi, je ne suis pas allé(e) en ville. Je n'ai pas acheté de savon. Je n'ai pas acheté de dentifrice.

Vive la France!

(a) Saumur is a historic town which is situated on the banks of the (river) Loire half-way between Angers and Tours. It is very well-known all over the world for its wine, especially the sparkling white wine which resembles Champagne. But do you know that in Saumur there is also the National School of Horsemanship, where all horse enthusiasts can come to discover the unique universe of this prestigious school. The Cadre Noir (Black Squad) gives demonstrations every two weeks in summer. Families can come to see a demonstration for 45 euros.

(b)
1. Visiter Saumur est indispensable si tu aimes les **c**hevaux.
2. Saumur est située à 67 km d'**A**ngers et à 66 km de Tours.
3. Les cavaliers **d**onnent des carousels en été.
4. Le vin blanc de Saumur **r**essemble au Champagne.
5. L'art équestre s'appelle l'**e**quitation.

(c) C – A – D – R – E: Cadre

Chapitre 6

What was it like?

Exercice 6.1 – CD: 25

Dialogue
The Silver Box (continued)

Peter, Martine's English penfriend, is going to make his second visit.

Dad.   Listen, darling. Don't forget that Peter is going to come in October.
Mum.   Ah yes. Where does he live, exactly, in England?
Dad.   I don't recall. I have the school's paperwork here, in a desk drawer. Or perhaps in my briefcase...
Mum.   He's a nice boy. But he does not talk much!
Dad.   He is perhaps going to speak more this time. After all, he has been learning French for three years now!
Mum.   Yes, that's true. Martine says that he writes quite well.
Dad.   And Martine writes to Peter in English, is that right?
Mum.   Yes. She writes to him in English. Poor Peter! So, where does he live?
Dad.   I've found it. Peter Harrison, 17 Rubens Road, Epsom, Surrey.
Mum.   Where is it? It is in which region?
Dad.   Pf... In the south, I think. What did he say last year?
Mum.   I can't remember.
Papa.   Ah! Here are the kids! So, what's the news?
Martine.   Granny is going to help us. She's going to write to her friend in Belgium!
Dad.   In Belgium?
Georges.   Yes. She has a friend who is very old, like her, who used to live in the village when they were little. She's called Albertine Levy.
Martine.   But when she was speaking, she seemed sad. It's strange.

Exercice 6.2

1. Peter is coming from England in October.
2. He is Martine's penfriend.
3. She's a friend of granny.
4. She thinks she is living in Belgium.
5. She noticed that she seemed sad when talking about Albertine.

Exercice 6.3

The expressions in the dialogue ending in –ait or –aient are:

elle habitait	she used to live
elles étaient	they used to be; they were
elle parlait	she was speaking
elle avait l'air	she seemed

Exercice 6.4
1. She was speaking; she used to speak.
2. He was singing; he used to sing.
3. She was living; she used to live.
4. He was starting; he used to start.
5. She was walking; she used to walk.

Exercice 6.5

1.	chanter	2.	choisir	3.	attendre
je	chantais	je	choisissais	j'	attendais
tu	chantais	tu	choisissais	tu	attendais
il	chantait	il	choisissait	il	attendait
elle	chantait	elle	choisissait	elle	attendait
nous	chantions	nous	choisissions	nous	attendions
vous	chantiez	vous	choisissiez	vous	attendiez
ils	chantaient	ils	choisissaient	ils	attendaient
elles	chantaient	elles	choisissaient	elles	attendaient

Exercice 6.6
1. J'arrivais à neuf heures du matin.
2. C'était agréable.
3. Mamie parlait aux enfants.
4. Son amie s'appelait Albertine.
5. Martine avait chaud.
6. Peter ne parlait pas beaucoup.
7. Georges et Martine n'allaient pas souvent chez Mamie.
8. Quand elle marchait, c'était difficile.
9. Il faisait beau et chaud en été.

Exercice 6.7
1. Je suis allé à Angers: c'était formidable!
2. Hier soir on a dîné au restaurant: c'était délicieux!
3. J'ai fait les magasins avec Martine: c'était amusant!
4. Nous avons fait du ski dans les Alpes: c'était passionnant!
5. On a visité le Musée du Louvre: c'était intéressant!

Here are some suggestions for numbers 6 to 10:

6. Nous sommes allés à Nantes: c'était amusant.
7. J'ai regardé un film à la télé: c'était passionnant.
8. Papa a fait de la planche à voile: c'était bizarre.
9. La semaine dernière nous avons fait du camping: c'était affreux.
10. Ma soeur est partie en avion: c'était sympa.

Exercice 6.8

Pupils are required to make sentences beginning with **J'étais...** (I used to be) and an adjective or two, and finishing with: **maintenant je suis...** (now I am), and another adjective. Girls should use feminine forms of the adjectives they choose.

For example:
J'étais faible et embêtant(e), maintenant je suis gentil(le)!
I was weak and annoying, now I am nice!

Exercice 6.9 – CD: 26

Dialogue

Martine. Hello granny. So, you have received a letter?
Mamie. Yes, I've received a letter.
Georges. So?
Mamie. It's not Albertine who wrote the letter.
Martine. Why? Is she dead?
Mamie. Certainly not! But she no longer lives in Belgium.
Georges. Brilliant! She has come back to France!
Mamie. Not that, either. She has emigrated.
Martine. Emigrated? Damn!
Mamie. It's a neighbour, who wrote to me.
Georges. What does he say, the neighbour? Where is she?
Mamie. The neighbour has lost her address. But you never know...

Exercice 6.10

1. Tu as reçu?
2. Ce n'est pas Albertine qui a écrit la lettre.
3. Pourquoi?
4. Elle est morte?
5. Elle n'habite plus en Belgique.
6. Elle est revenue.
7. Qui m'a écrit.
8. Qu'est-ce qu'il dit?
9. Le voisin a perdu son adresse.
10. On ne sait jamais...

Exercice 6.11

1. Il a reçu?
2. Ce n'est pas Martine qui a perdu l'adresse.
3. Elle est française?
4. Nous n'habitons plus en Angleterre.
5. Elles sont revenues.
6. Qui m'a lu.
7. Qu'est-ce qu'ils pensent?
8. Le voisin n'a pas perdu le journal.
9. On ne trouve jamais les réponses.

Exercice 6.12

Pupils are required to read out the French, to get used to the sound of the pronoun positions, then translate the phrases. Here are the translations:

1. You (sing.) look at me.
2. He looks for us.
3. She listens to you.
4. I speak to you.
5. He finds the exercise books there.
6. You (pl.) are listening to us.
7. We hear you.
8. I write to them.
9. You (sing.) send a letter to him / to her.
10. She asks us a question.

Exercice 6.13

Here are ten sample sentences:

1. Ils nous regardent. — They look at us.
2. Tu les regardes. — You look at them.
3. Je te regarde. — I look at you.
4. Nous vous regardons. — We look at you.
5. Elles les regardent. — They (f.) look at them.
6. Il me regarde. — He looks at me.
7. On la regarde. — One (We, They) look(s) at her / it.
8. Elle nous regarde. — She looks at us.
9. Je vous regarde. — I look at you.
10. Vous le regardez. — You (pl.) look at him / it.

Exercice 6.14

Here are ten example sentences:

1. Ils nous aident. — They help us.
2. Tu les aimes. — You (sing.) like them.
3. Je t'écoute. — I listen to you.
4. Nous vous prenons. — We take you.
5. Elles les mettent. — They put them (on).
6. Il m'aide. — He helps me.
7. On la prend. — One takes it (her).
8. Elle nous aime. — She likes us.
9. Je vous écoute. — I listen to you.
10. Vous le mettez. — You put it (on).

Note: 'se' has the most meanings; 'les' has the fewest.

Exercice 6.15

1. Le restaurant est plus grand que le café.
2. Marie est plus grande que Pierre.
3. Ton frère est plus petit que ma soeur.
4. A Paris il fait plus chaud qu'à Londres.
5. Février est plus froid qu'août.
6. Georges est plus loyal que Martine.
7. La ferme est plus belle que le parking.
8. Madame Lacroix est plus stricte que Monsieur Béchet.
9. Oui, mais elle est moins tolérante que Madame Schmidt.
10. Notre maison est aussi moderne que ton / votre appartement.

Exercice 6.16 – CD: 27

Dialogue

Mamie. Oh yes. It's no longer like before.
Martine. What, granny? What is no longer like before?
Mamie. Everything. Everything has changed. Everyone has gone, the village is different.
Georges. What was it like, granny, when you were young?
Mamie. Well, to start with, there was no motorway! Then, everything was calm. Everyone knew one another, everyone said hello to one another.
Georges. But, the village was different?
Mamie. Oh yes. There was no swimming pool, there were no shops.
Martine. No shops? But...
Mamie. There was the mayor's office, a little café, and a bakery.
Georges. Was there the car park, next to the church?
Mamie. A car park? There was only one car! The doctor had a car, but we went along on bikes or horseback.
Martine. I'm beginning to understand. It's different nowadays. Now we have two car parks, traffic lights, a village hall, a little kindergarten, a general store...
Mamie. All the young people used to work at the big farm.
Martine. The Big Farm? The restaurant?
Mamie. Of course not! It was a real farm in those days! We were in a farming region.

Exercice 6.17

Here are some examples of each comparative expression with the adjectives given. Pupils must make 5 sentences of their own.

1. Le village est plus intéressant que la ferme.
   The village is more interesting than the farm.
2. Martine est moins loyale que Georges.
   Martine is less loyal than Georges.
   (Martine is not as loyal as Georges).
3. Monsieur Béchet est aussi stricte que Madame Schmidt.
   Mr. Béchet is as strict as Mrs. Schmidt.
4. Mamie est moins active que Martine.
   Mamie is less active than Martine.
5. Le café est plus moderne que l'église.
   The café is more modern than the church.

Exercice 6.18 - CD: 28

Dialogue

Mamie.   Before, there were all sorts of festivities in the village. We were not rich, but we knew how to enjoy ourselves!
Martine.   But there are still festivities. There's the village festival, on the 1st June...
Mamie.   The village festival, that's not a real festival!
Martine.   Yes it is! There's a carousel, and a boules competition, and in the evening there's a disco for the young ones.
Mamie.   But when we were young, we had the feast of the sardine, the feast of the mogette (Vendée beans), the Mussels and Chips evening! And there were musicians who came to play, and we danced. It was nicer than today.
Georges.   The feast of the sardine?
Mamie.   Yes. It was excellent. The whole village came and sat at long tables. Sardines freshly cooked on charcoal grills were served and we used to eat and drink wine...
Georges.   So you had a really good time then granny?
Mamie.   Oh yes, we had a good time!

Exercice 6.19 - CD: 29

Reading passage.

That day, granny went on telling the children all about the village festivities of her youth. The children listened carefully. While she spoke, Martine and Georges tried to imagine the village in the past. Georges wanted to ask granny questions about the 1939 – 1945 war. Granny did not want to speak about this period. She only said that it was a sad time. But Martine wanted to know more. Once they got home, they spoke about granny and the silver box, about the village festivities, about Albertine Lévy and about the past. After dinner, Georges and Martine decided to do some research on the village. Martine suggested to her brother that they go to Nantes to look for information in the library.

1.   She went on talking about the village festivities of her youth.
2.   They listened attentively.
3.   She did not want to talk about the war because it was a sad period.
4.   Martine wanted to find out more.
5.   She suggested they go to the library in Nantes, to find more information about the village.

Exercice 6.20

1.   She is going to arrive in Nantes on the 21st April.
2.   We can do some research on the village.
3.   Mum wants to read the Sunday newspaper.
4.   We must take the 9.05 train.
5.   You continue to make progress.
6.   Dad begins to speak to M. Simonneau.
7.   We decide to stay at home.
8.   Martine promises to help Peter with his French.
9.   She tries to write to him in English.
10.   Peter is going to try to answer in French.

Exercice 6.21

1. Christian va aider maman dans le jardin.
2. Georges peut demander l'addition.
3. Martine veut aller à la bibliothèque à Nantes.
4. Je dois arriver avant le déjeuner.
5. Martine continue à faire un effort avec son anglais.
6. Elle commence à bien parler.
7. Peter veut apprendre le français en France.
8. Il va lire des journaux français.
9. Maman promet d'aider Georges avec ses devoirs.
10. Le frère de Martine va essayer de parler anglais avec Peter.

Vive la France!

You'll find the science park Futuroscope 11 km north of Poitiers, an important town in the centre-west of France. It is not only a theme park for young people, it's also an opportunity to experience powerful auditory and visual sensations, thanks to the ultra-modern technology which is constantly being updated. You can discover the latest developments in computing and science, in the ecology of the planet, and in space exploration.

(b)   POITIERS   ATTRACTIONS   PARC   SCIENCES   MODERNE

(c)   Pupils must find words of their own in the passage and jumble them up for their partner to decode.

Chapitre 7

The town centre, is it far?

Exercice 7.1 - CD: 30

Dialogue

Martine.	Gosh, there are so many people!
Georges.	Yes. Where is the library?
Martine.	I don't know. The last time that we came to Nantes I was three!
Georges.	Really?
Martine.	I have phoned Tochiko and asked her to come.
Georges.	Why?
Martine.	To help us.
Georges.	Great. Where are we meeting her?
Martine.	We arranged to meet at ten o'clock at the tourist office.
Georges.	Brilliant. But... where is the tourist office?
Martine.	Wait. What time is it?
Georges.	It is you who have the watch.
Martine.	You get on my nerves. Ouf! Here it is!. Its ten to ten.
Georges.	So, we have ten minutes.
Martine.	I have an intelligent brother.

Exercice 7.2

1. Georges et Martine veulent **trouver** la bibliothèque.
2. Martine **a** téléphoné à Tochiko.
3. A la gare, il y a **beaucoup** de **monde**.
4. Ils **vont** aller à l'office de tourisme.
5. Tochiko **va** être à l'office de **tourisme** à 9 h 50.
6. Martine **dit** qu'elle **a** un frère intelligent.

Exercice 7.3 - CD: 31

Dialogue

Martine.	I am going to ask this lady. Excuse me, how do we get to the tourist office, please?
Lady.	I am sorry. I am not from here. I don't know.

***

Martine.	Why don't you ask an employee?
Georges.	OK. Please sir, how do we get to the tourist office?
Employee.	There are two. The nearest is in Place du Maréchal Foch. Go left then turn right into rue Henri IV, go down the street, and then take the second street on the left and it's opposite the cathedral.
Georges.	Thank you sir.
Employee.	You're welcome.

***

Martine. Look! Here's Tochiko! Hi! How are you?
Tochiko. I'm fine. I have already asked for the directions. It's quite far, but it's easy. We need to take the tram, line 1, heading for Orvault, and get off at the university.
Martine. Fantastic. Shall we go?

Exercice 7.4

1. Go straight ahead. Take the second left. It's on your left. THE BAKER'S
2. Take the first left. Cross the Place Napoléon, and it's after the cinema on the left. THE CHURCH
3. Take the first left, cross the car park, carry on along the rue d'Austerlitz, then take the first on the right. It's opposite the post office. THE NEWSAGENT'S
4. Take the first left. Carry on for 150 metres. It's opposite the church. THE BANK

Exercice 7.5

1. Va tout droit, tourne à droite sur la rue d'Austerlitz, puis tourne à gauche. C'est sur la droite, à côté du parking.
2. Continue tout droit. Traverse la rue d'Austerlitz. C'est à gauche.
3. Continue tout droit et prends la première rue à droite. Tourne à droite. C'est à cinquante mètres, en face du cinéma.
4. Va tout droit et prends la première rue à droite. Traverse le parking, place Napoléon. C'est juste avant l'église, à gauche.
5. Continue tout droit sur cette rue. Après la rue d'Austerlitz, c'est à droite, en face de la poste.

Exercice 7.6

1. I tell mum to help me.
2. You ask dad to close the door.
3. She tells her brother to get up.
4. You ask the teacher to explain the lesson.
5. Martine tells Georges to speak to the employee.
6. I asked Pauline to give me some bread.
7. You have asked Paul's brother to go with you (accompany you)?
8. Tochiko asked the employee to give her a leaflet.
9. The policeman told Georges to take the first on the right.
10. Marie-Claire has asked Philippe's sister to come to the house.

Exercice 7.7

1. Maman dit à Georges d'ouvrir la fenêtre.
2. Tochiko demande au garçon d'apporter du pain.
3. L'agent dit à Martine de prendre la deuxième rue à droite.
4. Elle demande à l'employé de donner un dépliant à son frère.
5. Georges demande à son père de l'aider.
6. Marie-Claire a dit à son frère de passer le sel.
7. Pauline a demandé au prof d'expliquer.
8. Le prof lui a dit de regarder dans son livre.
9. Elles ont demandé à leurs amies de les accompagner.
10. Nous avons dit à la soeur de Georges de venir chez nous.

Exercice 7.8 CD: 32

Reading passage.

At the library.

Martine, Georges and Tochiko went out of the tourist office and took the tram to the library. After ten minutes, they arrived at the university, where they got off. They asked a student the way to the library. Inside, they quickly found a big book with the history of their village. It was very interesting, and they spent two hours studying the history of the village in the 1940s. The village was occupied by the Germans at that time. At first, everything was quite quiet. There was only one young soldier in the village. But later, the situation became difficult. The Germans deported lots of young men to go to work in Germany. Martine found a list of the people deported. On the list she read the name: Lévy, Jean-Paul. They found Tochiko and all three went out of the library. They bought bus tickets and returned to the town centre by bus, where they decided to have lunch at MacDonald's.

Exercice 7.9

1. Ils ont pris le tramway.
2. Ils sont descendus.
3. Ils ont demandé à un étudiant.
4. A l'intérieur.
5. Ils ont vite trouvé.
6. Ils ont passé deux heures à étudier.
7. Pendant les années 40.
8. Au début.
9. Elle a lu le nom.
10. Des tickets de bus.

Exercice 7.10

Cher Peter,   La Roche, le 10 juin

The answer to the letter should include the following:

1. Mes parents vont très bien merci.
2. En France, en ce moment, il fait beau et chaud.
3. Moi aussi j'aime quand il fait chaud, mais pas trop chaud!
4. La semaine dernière je suis allé à Nantes chercher des informations sur notre village pendant les années 40.
5. Je suis allé avec Martine.

Ecris-moi vite,

Ton ami, Georges.

Exercice 7.11

1. Elles vont
2. Elle trouve
3. Nous cherchons
4. Je tourne
5. Vous continuez
6. On lit
7. Ils font
8. Tu demandes
9. Il traverse
10. Elles prennent
11. Elle ne va pas
12. Vous ne trouvez pas
13. Je ne lis pas
14. Vous ne tournez pas
15. Nous ne traversons pas
16. Fais-tu? / Est-ce que tu fais?
17. Cherche-t-il? / Est-ce qu'il cherche?
18. Prenons-nous? / Est-ce que nous prenons?
19. Demande-t-elle? / Est-ce qu'elle demande?
20. Trouves-tu? / Trouvez-vous? / Est-ce que tu trouves? / Est-ce que vous trouvez?

Exercice 7.12

1. Elle est allée à Nantes.
2. Nous avons trouvé un gros livre d'histoire.
3. Tu as continué le long de la rue Grimaldi.
4. Vous avez tourné à droite après le cinéma.
5. Je suis allé(e) à la maison de la presse.
6. Nous avons fait des recherches.
7. Vous avez trouvé des informations?
8. Tu as pris des photos.
9. On a traversé la Place Napoléon.
10. Tu as lu le journal régional.
11. On a choisi le roman policier.
12. Vous avez allumé la télévision.
13. Philippe a demandé un plan.
14. Il est entré dans l'office de tourisme.
15. Nous avons fini le petit déjeuner.
16. Des touristes sont arrivés à la rivière.
17. Marie-Claude a posé des questions.
18. Maman a écrit une liste.
19. Les deux enfants ont fait du shopping.
20. Tu as écouté la radio ce matin.

Exercice 7.13

1. Tu vas chercher des informations.
2. Maman va attendre à la maison avec papa.
3. Martine va lire les instructions à la bibliothèque.
4. Georges ne va pas prendre de photos.
5. Ils vont aller à l'université en tramway.
6. Tochiko va rencontrer ses amis à l'office de tourisme.
7. Martine et Georges vont trouver l'histoire intéressante.
8. Le frère de Tochiko ne va pas venir souvent à Nantes.
9. Georges va être fatigué.
10. On va manger au MacDonald's.

Exercice 7.14

1. Tu cherchais.
2. Maman attendait.
3. Martine lisait.
4. Georges ne prenait pas.
5. Ils allaient.
6. Tochiko rencontrait.
7. Martine et Georges trouvaient.
8. Le frère de Tochiko ne venait pas.
9. Georges était.
10. On mangeait.

Exercice 7.15

1. C'est un café.
2. C'est une université.
3. C'est un tramway.
4. Ce sont des photos.
5. C'est une bibliothèque.
6. C'est une piscine.
7. C'est le cinéma.
8. C'est une boulangerie.
9. C'est l'office de tourisme.
10. C'est la gare (SNCF).

Exercice 7.16

Pupils have to design their own ideal French town in map form, using the vocabulary given on page 101.

Exercice 7.17

Pupils must use their own map to give directions to their partner, who must then say where they have been sent.

Exercice 7.18

Translation of the example given in the pupils' book:

A. Is there a cinema near here please?
B. There are two cinemas. The Dragon and the Rex.
A. Er... the Dragon.
B. Walk past the Town Hall, then turn left.
A. Thank you. Is it far?
B. No.

Vive la France!

(a) Do you like music? Do you like drama or dance? In summer there are all sorts of festivals all over France. In general, they last one or two weeks. There are festivals of classical music, modern music, opera, jazz, drama and dance; in short, all types of entertainment. In the south of France, it is possible to go to open-air concerts as in Aix-en-Provence or Nîmes, where performances are put on in the Roman arenas. In every town and village in France, you can find a concert, either in the local church or the village hall, not to mention the International Film Festival in Cannes where all the great filmstars come together!

(b) Pupils are asked to design a poster on paper or on the computer for a concert or other show in France. They must give dates, times and prices (in euros).

(c) The French word festival adds 's' in the plural – les festivals, unlike most words ending in –al, which change –al to –aux.

Chapitre 8

Let's hit the shops!

Exercice 8.1 – CD: 33

Martine. There! That's it! We've found the answer!
Georges. What answer?
Tochiko. I was told your brother was intelligent?
Martine. It isn't true.
Georges. What answer?
Martine. The meaning of the letters J-P.L. – you know – on the silver box!
Georges. Oh yes. Well, who is it?
Martine and Tochiko. Jean-Paul Lévy!
Georges. Yes. It's possible, but...
Martine. Georges, you are impossible.
Georges. I know.
Tochiko. And now, let's hit the shops! What time is it?
Martine. Wait. It's... a quarter to three.
Tochiko. Perfect! We'll go window-shopping and... who knows?

Pupils are asked to work in threes and present the above dialogue to the class.

Exercice 8.2

1. He does not initially understand what 'answer' the girls have found.
2. She says she had been told he was intelligent.
3. It is the meaning of the initials J-P.L.
4. He thinks it might be possible.
5. They are going to go shopping.
6. She says 'parfait' because there will be time to do some serious shopping!

Exercice 8.3

Pupils have to write a postcard from Nantes in French to a French friend. Here are some examples of phrases they could include using the clues they are given:

Il fait très beau ici.
The weather is fine here.

On est venus / Je suis venu(e) à Nantes par le train. C'est confortable et rapide.
We came / I came to Nantes by train. It's comfortable and fast.

Je suis allé(e) / On est allés au centre ville en tramway, parce que c'est facile. Ce n'est pas cher!
I went / We went to the town centre by tram, because it's easy. It's not expensive!

J'ai visité / On a visité le château. C'était magnifique.
I visited / We visited the chateau. It was magnificent.

J'ai mangé / On a mangé au MacDo.
I ate / We ate at MacDonald's.

J'ai acheté des cartes postales.
I bought some postcards.

Exercice 8.4 - CD: 34

Dad.   Hello?
Martine.   Hello Dad, it's me.
Dad.   Hi sweetheart. Where are you?
Martine.   In Nantes. That's it. We've done it!
Dad.   Really? And?
Martine.   I'll tell you everything when we get home. We've just eaten and we are going to go shopping.
Dad.   OK. Call me when you get to the station? Great. See you later!

***

Mum.   Well?
Dad.   It seems that they have found something. Martine is over the moon!
Mum.   Fantastic. I am just making coffee. Would you like some?
Dad.   Of course!

Exercice 8.5

1. mettant
2. sonnant
3. appelant
4. finissant
5. vendant
6. lisant
7. choisissant
8. partant
9. ouvrant
10. rangeant

Exercice 8.6

1. En regardant
2. En mettant
3. En trouvant
4. En partant
5. En faisant
6. En écoutant la radio
7. En voyageant à Nantes
8. En demandant un plan
9. En regardant la télévision
10. En recevant ta lettre

Exercice 8.7

1. En écoutant la radio, j'ai chanté.
   While listening to the radio, I sang.
2. En faisant la cuisine, papa a regardé la télévision.
   While doing the cooking, dad watched television.
3. En voyageant à Nantes, Martine a lu un magazine pour les ados.
   While travelling to Nantes, Martine read a teenage magazine.
4. En arrivant à la bibliothèque, Georges a demandé des directions.
   On arriving at the library, Georges asked for directions.
5. En entrant dans la salle de bains, je suis tombé(e).
   On going into the bathroom, I fell.

Exercice 8.8 – CD: 35

Martine. By the way, Tochiko, do want to buy some clothes?
Tochiko. Maybe. But I'm mainly looking for souvenirs of Nantes.
Georges. Me too. Shall we buy a present for granny?
Martine. Of course. Right, we need to find a gift and souvenir shop.
Tochiko. I've been told that there are some pretty shops in the little streets near the château.
Martine. That's right. We can go there on foot. It is not far. How much pocket money do you get, usually?
Tochiko. It depends. Ten, fifteen euros a week. But I have to do chores!
Georges. So do we. I wash the car or mow the lawn.
Martine. I do the shopping for the neighbours from time to time.
Tochiko. Oh. I help mum to do the housework.

***

Tochiko. There. We have arrived. "The Golden Gift". Shall we go in?
Martine. Of course. There's everything here!
Georges. I wanted to buy a t-shirt, but they are expensive.
Martine. Yes. But there are some nice key-rings, or caps.
Tochiko. I'm going to buy a little bottle of perfume for my mother. And sweets for my brothers and sisters!
Martine. Madame, excuse me, this red t-shirt: how much is it?
Saleswoman. This one with the boat on it?
Martine. No. That one behind it.
Saleswoman. Thirteen euros, mademoiselle.

An hour later, at the train station...

Tochiko. Good. There's our train. It leaves in two minutes! We must hurry!
Martine. The tickets! We haven't validated our ticktets!

Exercice 8.9

1. She has just telephoned granny.
2. We have just eaten in a restaurant.
3. Martine has just paid for her t-shirt.

4. You've just got up? But it's already 10 o'clock!
5. Dad is reading his paper.
6. Mum is getting lunch ready.
7. You are choosing some souvenirs.
8. M. Simonneau was gardening.
9. When I arrived, mum was reading a magazine.
10. Tochiko is tidying her bedroom.

Exercice 8.10

1. Je viens de me lever.
2. Nous venons de prendre le déjeuner.
3. Elle est en train de lire.
4. Ils sont en train d'acheter des souvenirs.
5. Martine vient de choisir un T-shirt.
6. A trois heures moins le quart, papa était en train d'écouter la radio.
7. Martine était en train de boire du thé.
8. Tochiko vient de téléphoner à ses parents.
9. Je viens de trouver une histoire du village.
10. Georges est en train de choisir une casquette.

Exercice 8.11

1. Je viens de prendre le déjeuner.
2. Je viens de recevoir une lettre.
3. Je viens d' écrire à mes grands-parents.
4. Je viens de lire un article.
5. Je viens de me lever.
6. Je viens de regarder la télévision.
7. Je viens de discuter avec les ami(e)s.
8. Je viens d'écouter la radio.
9. Je viens de faire un dessin.
10. Je viens d'attendre le bus.

Exercice 8.12

1. Je suis en train de prendre le déjeuner.
2. Je suis en train de recevoir une lettre.
3. Je suis en train d' écrire à mes grands-parents.
4. Je suis en train de lire un article.
5. Je suis en train de me lever.
6. Je suis en train de regarder la télévision.
7. Je suis en train de discuter avec les ami(e)s.
8. Je suis en train d'écouter la radio.
9. Je suis en train de faire un dessin.
10. Je suis en train d'attendre le bus.

Exercice 8.13

Pupils are asked to mime actions for others to guess what they are in the process of doing, or what they have just done.

Exercice 8.14

1. En arrivant au magasin — (c) j'ai regardé les T-shirts et les autres souvenirs.
2. Quand papa est fatigué — (j) il ne veut pas discuter avec moi.
3. Je ne regarde pas la télévision — (e) quand j'ai mal aux yeux.
4. Elle est en train de lire le livre — (b) qu'elle a choisi ce matin.
5. Pourquoi n'as-tu pas ouvert — (h) le cadeau que je t'ai donné?
6. Peter va écrire en français et — (d) Martine va écrire en anglais.
7. En entrant dans l'office de tourisme — (i) j'ai demandé un dépliant sur la ville.
8. Les informations que je voulais — (g) n'étaient pas là.
9. Quel temps faisait-il en Italie — (f) quand vous étiez là en vacances?
10. A quelle heure va-t-on — (a) ouvrir le magasin de souvenirs?

Exercice 8.15 CD: 36

Dad. Martine has just phoned. They are about to arrive at the station.
Mum. You are going to go and get them?
Dad. Of course! Are you coming with me?
Mum. No. I'm staying here.
Dad. Don't forget that I'm doing the cooking tonight!
Mum. Don't worry! I haven't forgotten!

***

Martine. Hi mum!
Mum. But... where is Tochiko?
Georges. Her dad came to fetch her at the station.
Mum. What a pity! I was expecting her for supper.
Georges. I think that it's her mother's birthday.
Dad. So, what's the news?
Martine. I think we have discovered the owner of the little box.
Mum. But that is incredible! So who is it?
Georges. It's a war deportee from the village who is called Jean-Paul Lévy. There was a list. He was the only "J-P.L.".
Mum. It's possible, but he must have died by now.
Martine. But he must have some family. Albertine?
Georges. Yes! She is perhaps Jean-Paul's wife!
Mum. They were very young.
Dad. Or his sister?
Mum. How are we going to know?

Pupils must prepare and present the above dialogue to the class.

Exercice 8.16

1. Martine telephoned when they were about to arrive at the station.
2. That dad is doing the cooking tonight.
3. Because she has gone home for her mother's birthday.
4. She thinks that they were too young at the time.
5. She asks how they are going to find out more.

Exercice 8.17

| TRAMWAY | BUS | TRAIN | LIGNE | TICKET |
| COMPOSTER | MACDO | PARFUM | CASQUETTE | CADEAU |

Exercice 8.18

The correct order for the sentences is:

6. Je me suis levé.
3. Je suis descendu et j'ai préparé mon petit déjeuner.
5. J'ai pris des céréales, du jus d'orange et du café.
8. Quand j'ai quitté la maison, il était huit heures cinq.
2. Je suis allé à la gare à pied, parce qu'il faisait beau.
4. En arrivant à la gare, j'ai acheté un ticket, et je l'ai composté.
1. Je suis arrivé à mon bureau, mais il était fermé!
7. C'était le weekend!

Exercice 8.19 CD: 37

Dictée

Je m'appelle Marie. / J'habite à Paris. / Hier ma mère et ma soeur sont allées en ville. / Ma soeur est intelligente et belle. / Moi, je suis nulle en classe, / et je ne parle pas beaucoup.

Vive le France!

This bridge is part of the extraordinary aqueduct constructed by the Romans to bring water from the spring of La Fontaine d'Eure at Uzès as far as the town of Nîmes, a distance of nearly fifty kilometres. The Pont du Gard is, today, the most visited ancient monument in France. Its construction, which probably took about 15 years, was finished under the emperor Trajan between the years 60 and 70 AD. Made up of three rows of superposed arches, it is 49 metres high.

(b)
1. fait partie de
2. construit par
3. un parcours de
4. s'est achevée
5. de notre ère (literally: of our era, i.e., in 'our' time)

(c)
1. J'ai visité le Pont du Gard l'année dernière.
2. C'est une magnifique construction antique.
3. Les Romains ont construit le pont.
4. L'aqueduc conduit l'eau d'Uzès à Nîmes.
5. Il y a trois étages d'arches.

Chapitre 9

Revision of Book I

Exercice 9.1

France and Europe – some statistics.

France has a population of sixty million inhabitants, that is to say 108 inhabitants per square kilometre. In Belgium, there are ten million, four hundred thousand inhabitants, a population density of 340 inhabitants per square kilometre. In Switzerland, French is spoken in the west of the country, and in Luxembourg French is one of the three official languages. Jacques Chirac has been President of the Republic since 1995. The French currency has been the euro since 2002. Seventy-five per cent of French people live in towns, nine and a half million of them in Paris.

1. c'est-à-dire
2. par kilomètre carré
3. dans l'ouest du pays
4. la monnaie française
5. pour cent

Exercice 9.2

1. France: population = 60.000.000
2. France: densité de population = 108 habitants / km^2
3. Belgique: population = 10.400.000
4. Belgique: densité de population = 340 habitants / km^2
5. Date de la première élection de J. Chirac = 1995
6. Date de la mise en circulation de l'euro = 2002
7. Population urbaine (%) = 75%
8. Population de Paris = 9.500.000

Exercice 9.3

1. connexion — féminin
2. voisine — féminin
3. dépôt — masculin
4. vigne — féminin
5. valise — féminin
6. nuage — masculin
7. tasse — féminin
8. cafetière — féminin
9. tapis — masculin
10. marteau — masculin.

Exercice 9.4

1. Christian et Elodie **ont** deux enfants.
2. Martine **est** la soeur de Georges.
3. La famille de Tochiko **est** nombreuse.
4. Philippe va au travail à vélo parce qu'il n'**a** pas de voiture.
5. Je **suis** professeur de français en Angleterre.
6. Mes cousins **sont** étudiants à l'université de Nantes.
7. Vous **avez** des cartes postales, madame?
8. Elles **sont** belles, ces casquettes bleues.
9. Tu **as** quel âge, Marie-Claire?
10. Nous **sommes** trois: mon père, ma soeur et moi.
11. Elle **a** une assez grande maison.
12. La maison **a** quatre chambres et deux salles de bain.
13. Où **sont** les journaux de papa?
14. On **a** un panorama sur toute la vallée.
15. Super! Vous **avez** de la chance.

Exercice 9.5

1. I'm thirteen.
2. My birthday is on the thirty-first of August.
3. My elder brother is older than my cousin.
4. Sandrine is going to be twelve on the third of February.
5. I have given her a present. / I gave her (him) a present.
6. The day before my birthday, we had a party.
7. The following day, I watched television.
8. My friend Jean-Christophe is eleven.
9. Caroline's children are nine and seven.
10. When I was fifteen, the village was quiet.

Exercice 9.6

1. D'habitude, nous **mangeons** à midi et quart.
2. Martine **ferme** les volets pour aider papa.
3. Vous **habitez** loin?
4. Tu **ranges** ta chambre, s'il te plaît.
5. Sophie et Anne-Marie **chantent** à l'église.
6. Marcel **couche** à l'école: c'est un pensionnat.
7. Je **voyage** en avion quand c'est possible.
8. Nous **travaillons** tous les soirs.
9. On **donne** de bonnes notes aux bons élèves.
10. Quelqu'un **sonne** à la porte.
11. Nous **parlons** au professeur de maths.
12. Tu **écoutes** souvent la radio le matin?
13. Normalement je **regarde** la télévision.
14. Papa **cherche** Martine et Georges à la gare.
15. Mes cousins étudient en France/

Exercice 9.7

1. On va **au** cinéma.
2. Nous allons manger **au** restaurant ce soir.
3. Tu es allée **à** Nantes Martine?
4. Thérèse a un magasin de mode **à** Saint-Mâlo.
5. J'ai donné du chocolat **aux** enfants.
6. Ils demandent des informations **à la** mairie.
7. J'ai téléphoné **au** frère de Jacques.
8. Martine a fait des cours de biologie **à l'**école.
9. La grand-mère a écrit une lettre **à** Albertine.
10. Tu veux aller **à la** piscine?

Exercice 9.8

1. à la piscine
2. à l'église
3. à la salle de classe
4. à l'école
5. à la maison / chez moi
6. à Paris
7. chez Martine
8. chez le pharmacien / à la pharmacie
9. aux animaux
10. à la gare

Exercice 9.9

1. C'est **mon** frère.
2. Comment il s'appelle, **ton** frère?
3. **Ma** soeur a quinze ans.
4. Où sont **tes** stylos?
5. Ils sont dans **ma** trousse.
6. **Mes** parents n'aiment pas le poisson.
7. J'adore **sa** maison.
8. **Son** frère a deux vélos.
9. Tu as perdu **ta** bicyclette?
10. Comment s'appelle **sa** mère?

Exercice 9.10

The corrected mistakes are highlighted in **bold type**:
(Note to teachers: The Pupil's book contains seven errors not six as indicated and are as follows.)

Mon copain **s'appelle** Jules. Il **habite** en ville avec **sa** soeur et leur **cousin** Charles. Ils vont en voiture **à la** campagne, où ils font un pique-nique au bord de la rivière. A la maison, Jules, Rachel et Charles regardent la télévision de Charles. **Sa** télévision est très **petite**.

Chapitre 9

Exercice 9.11

My friend is called Jules. He lives in town with his sister and their cousin Charles. On Sundays they go by car to the country, where they have a picnic by the riverside. At home, Jules, Rachel and Charles watch Charles's television. His television is very small.

Exercice 9.12

The **Infinitives** of the verbs in the list are:

se coucher	to go to bed, to lie down
se lever	to get up
s'arrêter	to stop
se dépêcher	to hurry
s'habiller	to get dressed
se réveiller	to wake up
se demander	to wonder
s'ennuyer	to get bored
se laver	to wash / to wash oneself

Exercice 9.13

1. Nous nous couchons de bonne heure.
2. Tu te dépêches!
3. Vous vous réveillez tôt le matin.
4. Marcel s'ennuie facilement.
5. Je me demande s'il sait nager.
6. On s'habille en noir.
7. Elles se lèvent quand le prof entre dans le labo.
8. Elle ne s'arrête pas à la frontière, ce n'est pas nécessaire.
9. Tu t'approches du village.
10. Je me baigne avant de déjeuner.

Exercice 9.14

A neuf heures, je **me lève**. Je **fais** mon lit et je **me lave**. Je **nettoie** la salle de bains, et je **range** ma chambre. Je **mets** mes affaires de classe dans mon sac à dos et mes vêtements dans mon armoire. Je **mets** mes CDs et mes livres dans les tiroirs de mon bureau et je **sors** de ma chambre. Je **descends** dans la cuisine où je **prépare** mon petit déjeuner. Il **est** huit heures. Je **pars** à l'école.

Exercice 9.15

1. fourchette (fork)   The others are rooms.
2. entrée (entrance)   The others are animals.
3. cheval (horse)   The others are types of road or landscape features.
4. stylo (pen)   The others are musical instruments.
5. livre (book)   The others are all school subjects.

Exercice 9.16

1. Je ne trouve pas mes affaires de classe.
2. Tu n'as pas de trousse bleue.
3. Nous ne mangeons pas au restaurant chinois.
4. Tu n'as pas mon pull maman?
5. Il ne cherche pas ses livres de bandes dessinées.
6. On n'a pas de romans en anglais.
7. Nous n'avons pas de maison en Bretagne.
8. Pierre ne va pas à La Rochelle.
9. Tochiko n'habite pas à Nantes.
10. Charles ne tond pas la pelouse.

Exercice 9.17

1. mardi trois août   or   mardi 3 août.
2. mercredi vingt janvier   or   mercredi 20 janvier.
3. jeudi quatorze juillet   or   jeudi 14 juillet.
4. le premier avril   or   le 1er avril.
5. samedi dix-neuf mars   or   samedi 19 mars.

Exercice 9.18

Je vais aller de Calais à Paris **par le train**. De là, je vais partir **en TGV** jusqu'à Lyon, où je vais parcourir la ville **en taxi** et **à pied**. Puis je vais explorer les vieux quartiers **à vélo**. Je vais descendre dans un petit hôtel pas cher. Le lendemain, je vais continuer à découvrir ce pays **en car** avant de retourner en Angleterre **en avion**.

1. aller.
2. de là.
3. partir.
4. parcourir la ville.
5. les vieux quartiers.
6. descendre dans un petit hôtel pas cher.
7. à découvrir ce pays.
8. avant de retourner.

Exercice 9.19

1. Nous achetons des souvenirs.
2. Tu achètes du parfum pour maman.
3. Elle se promène dans les bois.
4. Je me lève à sept heures.
5. Ils achètent des CDs.
6. Nous jetons les papiers dans la poubelle.
7. Il s'appelle Peter, n'est-ce pas?
8. Tu jettes les feuilles, et tu gardes les carottes.
9. Si tu arrives lundi, tu m'appelles.
10. J'appelle Nicolas tous les jours.

Exercice 9.20

1. Est-elle à la maison?   Est-ce qu'elle est à la maison?
2. Aimez-vous Brahms?   Est-ce que vous aimez Brahms?
3. Voulez-vous aller à Paris?   Est-ce que vous voulez aller à Paris?

4.	Mange-t-on des escargots en Grande-Bretagne?		Est-ce qu'on mange des escargots en Grande-Bretagne?
5.	Aiment-ils les crêpes?		Est-ce qu'ils aiment les crêpes?
6.	Veux-tu apprendre à parler français?		Est-ce que tu veux apprendre à parler français?
7.	Peut-elle venir avec nous?		Est-ce qu'elle peut venir avec nous?
8.	Est-ce que Nathalie achète des souvenirs?*		
9.	Peut-on voir les animaux à la ferme?		Est-ce qu'on peut voir les animaux à la ferme?
10.	As-tu froid?		Est-ce que tu as froid?

*With names, in conversation, use Est-ce que.

Exercice 9.21

1. Tu as raison.
2. J'ai froid et j'ai faim.
3. Mais je n'ai pas peur.
4. Et toi?
5. Est-ce que tu as peur?
6. As-tu soif?

Exercice 9.22

1. Elle va voyager.
2. Nous allons lire des romans.
3. Ils vont arriver à 15 h.
4. Il va coûter 4 €.
5. Pourquoi allez-vous en voiture?
6. Quand va-t-il rentrer à la maison?
7. Elles ne vont pas se lever tôt.
8. Nous allons regarder un film à la télévision.
9. Je vais partir à 20 h.
10. Mais le film va commencer à 19 h 55!

Vive la France!

(a) The Principality of Monaco is situated on the French Riviera. It's a quasi-independent State surrounded by the department of Alpes-Maritimes. Its 30,000 inhabitants, who are known as Monégasques, live on the 1.95 km^2 of this constitutional monarchy, which is 3 kilometres long by 300 metres wide. The territory is dominated by Mount Agel (1,100 metres). Prince Rainier, head of the Grimaldi royal family, died in 2005 and his son, Prince Albert, became Head of State in his place. Millions of French people and other Europeans are interested in the family life of the Grimaldis. You can read articles about this family in French and foreign glossy magazines almost every week. The State owes its fortune to tourism and to its casino, but what everyone loves most is to find out more about Caroline, Stephanie and the joys and woes of this monarchy which sits within a republic.

(b) Pupils must write a letter in French to their teacher detailing an imaginary visit to the Royal Palace of Monaco, where they have been invited to spend three days.

(c) Pupils are asked to draw a plan of their 'ideal palace or chateau', in which all the rooms and other parts of the property are labelled in French. The internet could provide lots of ideas for this project.

Chapitre 10

Revision of Book II
Exercice 10.1 – CD: 38
Childhood Memories

In the spring, when the weather was fine, I used to like to go out very early in the morning to walk bare-footed in the orchard on the other side of the road. It was wonderful to be woken by the first rays of the sun, and to feel at the same time the still-icy dawn dew in the grass under the pear and apple trees. After half-an-hour, I used to come back in quietly through the kitchen door. I used to go back to my room, which was on the ground floor, and snuggle in my bed which was still warm. Ten minutes later, I would hear my father going downstairs to make coffee for mum, who was dozing in her bed.

1. It was spring time.
2. The orchard was across the road from the house.
3. We know the writer is a girl because there is an extra –e on réveillée.
4. She had gone out through the kitchen door.
5. It was on the ground floor.

Exercice 10.2

1. Quand il faisait beau.
2. Très tôt le matin.
3. Les premiers rayons du soleil.
4. Au bout d'une demi-heure.
5. J'entendais mon père qui descendait.

Exercice 10.3

1. Quand il faisait froid.
2. Très tard l'après-midi.
3. Les derniers rayons du soleil.
4. Au bout d'une heure et demie.
5. Elle voyait sa mère qui montait.

Exercice 10.4

1. faisait
2. aimais
3. était
4. rentrais
5. retrouvais
6. était
7. me réfugiais
8. entendais
9. descendait
10. somnolait

Ces verbes sont à l'imparfait parce que c'est une description au passé et que la fille faisait ces choses beaucoup de fois, régulièrement, dans le passé.

These verbs are in the imperfect because it is a description in the past, and because the girl did these things many times, regularly, in the past.

Exercice 10.5

1. Je prends le bus à 10 h.
2. Elle boit de l'orangina quand il fait chaud.
3. Nous partons à midi.
4. Elles dorment l'après-midi.
5. Il sort tous les soirs.

6. Le vendeur a servi le client
7. Martine a bu le café.
8. Tu n'as pas pris le tramway samedi.
9. Ont-ils bien dormi?
10. Elle est partie à 22 h 00 hier.

11. Le mardi, je prenais le petit déjeuner à 8 h 00.
12. Tous les matins, elle sortait.
13. Ils buvaient.
14. Vous dormiez.
15. La serveuse servait le déjeuner.

Exercice 10.6 – CD: 39
Dictée

Cet après-midi, / le facteur est arrivé / avec le courrier. / Il faisait beau, / mais le facteur portait toujours son gros manteau. / Après avoir déposé trois lettres, / il est parti / sans me parler. / Ce n'est pas la première fois / qu'il a fait froid. / D'habitude les facteurs s'arrêtent / et passent quelques minutes / à bavarder.

Exercice 10.7

The following is a translation of Christophe's e-mail:

> Hi Patrick!
> This morning I received a post card from my parents who are on holiday at the seaside. Yesterday evening they had dinner at Chez Jules restaurant in St Gilles. Do you know St Gilles? It's really nice! My mother had a seafood platter, and my father tried the skate cooked in butter. According to them it was delicious. I read the menu, the last time that they went there. Do you like fish? What did you eat the last time that you went to a restaurant? Thanks for the Geography file you sent me. It's just the thing.
> Cheers!
> Christophe

Pupils are required to put together an answer in French to this e-mail, imagining that they are Patrick.

Exercice 10.8

1. Il a reçu.
2. Nous avons reçu.
3. Mon frère, qui est à Paris.
4. Ma soeur, qui était en Angleterre.
5. Son oncle, qui était en vacances.
6. On a dîné.
7. Ils connaissent Londres.
8. Tu ne connais pas Nantes.
9. J'ai essayé le poulet rôti.
10. La première fois que tu es allé(e) en France.

Exercice 10.9

1. Je n'habite pas au bord de la mer.
2. Nous n'aimons pas les fruits de mer.
3. Tu n'as pas trouvé ton sac?
4. Je n'ai pas été malade.
5. Il n'avait pas mal au bras.
6. Elle n'est pas allée chez le médecin.
7. Nous ne sommes pas allés à la pharmacie.
8. On n'a pas d'ordonnance.
9. Je n'ai pas acheté de médicament.
10. Tu n'as pas suivi les instructions.

Exercice 10.10

1. Sait-il à quelle heure on part?
2. Est-ce que tu as mal à la gorge? / As-tu mal à la gorge?
3. Est-ce qu'elle a mal au dos?
4. Connaissez-vous la rue Picpus?
5. A-t-elle vu l'accident?
6. Est-ce que la dame est tombée par terre?
7. Est-ce que tu connaissais la victime?
8. Savait-il que j'étais malade?
9. Vas-tu aller à l'hôpital?
10. Est-ce qu'on arrive, papa?

Exercice 10.11

On a sonné à la porte. Je suis descendu. J'ai ouvert la porte et j'ai vu le facteur. Il m'a donné un paquet. Je suis entré dans la cuisine et j'ai ouvert le paquet. J'ai découvert un agenda pour l'année prochaine – un cadeau que ma tante m'a offert. J'ai décidé d'écrire des notes tous les jours.

Voici les premiers mots que j'ai écrits:

Aujourd'hui je me suis levé à 7 h 10, quand le courrier est arrivé.

Exercice 10.12

1. Je **les** trouve délicieuses.
2. Tu **les** écoutes ce soir?
3. On **le** regarde.
4. Vous **l'**avez?
5. Non. je ne **l'**ai pas.
6. Tu **le** vois?
7. Je **le** prépare.
8. Nous **les** regardons.
9. Elle **l'**oublie.
10. Il **le** déteste.

Exercice 10.13

1. Je nettoie
2. On essuie
3. Tu essaies
4. Vous achetez
5. Elle se lève
6. Nous mangeons
7. Tu te promènes
8. On jette
9. Ils s'appellent
10. J'achète

Exercice 10.14

1. J'ai nettoyé.
2. On a essuyé.
3. Tu as essayé.
4. Vous avez acheté.
5. Elle s'est levée.
6. Nous allons manger.
7. Tu vas te promener.
8. On va jeter.
9. Ils vont s'appeler.
10. Je vais acheter.

Exercice 10.15

The mistakes are indicated below in place, in their corrected form.

Je m'appelle Carlo. Je suis un garçon **italien**. La semaine **dernière**, je **suis** allé **chez le** médecin parce que j'**avais** mal **au** ventre. En plus, j'**étais** fatigué et j'**avais** mal **à la** tête.

Exercice 10.16 – CD: 40

Mamie. Hello?
Albertine. Florence? Is that you?
Mamie. Yes, it is me. Who is speaking?
Albertine. Florence! Don't you recognise my voice? It's Albertine!
Mamie. Albertine! Is it really you? It's not a joke? Where are you?
Albertine. But of course it's me! How are you?
Mamie. I'm all right. But where are you? Have you come back to Belgium?
Albertine. No! I live in Canada! A friend from Belgium found my phone number and... that's why!
Mamie. In Canada? Oh dear! What a long way away!
Albertine. By the way, my friend told me that a silver box has been found with "J-P.L." written on it. Is it true?
Mamie. Yes, it's true. A pretty little box. But who is J-P.L.?
Albertine. It's my brother. Listen, it's not a problem. I am going to come to see you in France at Christmas! Who found the box?
Mamie. It's M. Simonneau, my daughter's neighbour.
Albertine. Florence, can you give me the name of a good hotel?
Mamie. Don't be silly, you're going to stay with me!

1. Florence is granny's first name.
2. She does not believe it is really Albertine. — no, 1st, she doesn't know who it is
3. Her Belgian friend found her phone number and called her.
4. J-P.L. is Albertine's brother, Jean-Paul Lévy.
5. She's coming to France at Christmas.
6. She will be staying at granny's house.

Finding the French expression:

1. Bien sûr que c'est moi!
2. Où es-tu?
3. Que c'est loin!
4. Mon ami m'a dit.
5. Je vais venir vous voir.

Exercice 10.17

"What are you reading?"
"I'm not reading."
"What are you looking at?"
"I'm not looking at anything."
"You're not looking at anything?"
"I'm not reading anything, I'm not looking at anything."
"You never read?"
"Never. I never read anything"
"But you used to read."
"When I was little. But now I no longer read."
"So. You used to read, but now you never read anything any more. Is that right?"
"That's right!"

Exercice 10.18

1. Tu viens cet après-midi si tu veux.
2. Je ne peux pas.
3. Elle ne sait pas danser.
4. Le cambrioleur tient un revolver à la main.
5. Nous venons en voiture.

Exercice 10.19

1. Ecoutez le professeur!
2. Partons tout de suite!
3. Suivez-moi!
4. Prends-les!
5. Viens chez moi!
6. Sortez d'ici!
7. N'ayez pas peur!
8. Dépêchons-nous!
9. Ne vous disputez pas!
10. Sois sage!

Exercice 10.20

1. Je **lui** rends le devoir.
2. Nous **lui** envoyons une carte postale.
3. Mes parents **y** sont en vacances.
4. Tu **leur** passes le pain.
5. On **lui** demande.
6. Il **leur** donne les livres.
7. Vous **y** rentrez.
8. Ils **leur** envoient un message.
9. Nous **y** habitons depuis longtemps.
10. Paul s'**y** trouve.

Exercice 10.21

1. Je lui demande d'écrire.
2. Il me dit d'écouter.
3. Elle te demande de rester.
4. Ils nous disent de regarder.
5. Nous leur demandons d'écouter.
6. Vous me dites de venir mardi.
7. Elles lui demandent de partir.
8. Nous te disons de regarder.
9. Je lui demande d'attendre.
10. Il vous dit de commencer.

Exercice 10.22

She's called Stéphanie. She has two brothers – José and Arthur. José is 13 and Arthur is two years older than him. Stéphanie is younger (less old) than Arthur but older than José. Stéphanie also has a sister called Isabelle. Isabelle is as old as Stéphanie: they are twins.

Il s'appelle Jean. Il a douze ans. Il a un frère qui s'appelle Simon et une soeur qui s'appelle Charlotte. Simon est moins âgé que Jean de trois ans, mais Charlotte est plus âgée que Jean de trois ans. Charlotte est la plus grande. Elle est plus grande que Jean et plus grande que Simon. Simon est moins grand que Jean de 33 centimètres.

Exercice 10.23

Pupils make 2 drawings to illustrate what they have written in exercice 10.22.

Exercice 10.24

Pupils' letters must include:

	Examples:
when they arrived	je suis arrivé(e) le 4 juillet
by which method of transport	en avion; par le train; en voiture
what the **weather** is like	il fait beau; il fait chaud; il pleut
what they **have just done**	je viens de faire une promenade
what someone **is doing now**	mon père est en train de lire
what they **did** yesterday	hier j'ai visité le château
what they are **going to do** tomorrow	demain je vais aller en ville

Exercice 10.25

Pupils must make a board game designed to help them with their French revision. French only should be used.

Vive la France!

(a) Are you interested in football? Lots of people know the name of at least one French football team: Paris-Saint-Germain, Saint-Etienne, Nantes... Many more have heard of Thierry Henry, Zinedine Zidane and other French footballers. But what is the history of the sport in France? Here are a few key dates: 1872 saw the creation of the first French club, called Le Havre Athletic Club. The first match involving a national French team took place in Brussels in 1904 against Belgium, but the result was a bit disappointing: a three-all draw. In 1919 the French Football Federation was founded, and in 1921 Jules Rimet became President of FIFA.

From 1932 to 1933, the first professional championship was played. The winning team was Olympique Lillois. In 1938 France had the honour of organising the third World Cup, and in 1960 she hosted the first European Nations Championship.

On the 27th June 1984, France won the European Nations Championship, and on 12th July 1998, for the first time in its history, France won the World Cup. On the 2nd July 2000 France won the European Championship.

(b) Pupils have to write down the names of French footballers they know, then assemble their 'ideal French team'. This could be done as a group activity.

(c) Pupils design their own strip for the French national team to wear.